WINGS OF WAR

In *Flight to Arras*, Antoine de Saint-Exupéry condenses the high drama of months of combat flights into a single terrifying mission during the last dark days of the fall of France. In doing so, the man widely regarded as the greatest pilot-author of all time reveals his profound humanism.

Saint-Ex, as he was fondly known, was both a veteran pilot and a veteran survivor. He had fought the Moors in Africa, battled the roaring gales of Patagonia, and endured nearly drowning in the ocean and nearly dying of thirst in the desert. Although at first he did not consider himself to be a professional writer, he attained instant international literary success by vividly transferring to his books the emotions he felt while flying.

When war came in September 1939, Saint-Exupéry, an Air Force reserve officer, was called to active duty and assigned to training in long-range bombardment. Faced with a months-long course in an activity that he found repugnant and determined not to write about the war except as a participant, he exerted all of his persuasive charm to be transferred to combat duty. So at the age of thirty-nine, his body strewn with fractures and his left shoulder partially paralyzed from his many crashes, Saint-Exupéry returned to combat. His request for transfer had been granted only after being carried all the way to the office of the Air Minister.

Despite his desire to be a fighter pilot, he was assigned to Reconnaissance Group II/33, flying the beautiful but ineffective twin-engine Potez 637 aircraft. The famous writer, a big, clumsy bear of a man with a luminous smile and the ability to do almost supernaturally clever card tricks, was readily accepted by the other men. Yet until he had fulfilled the combat obligations that bound the aircrews together, Saint-Exupéry felt like an outsider. The concept of this desirable solidarity, earned only by doing one's duty, forms the philosophical basis for *Flight to Arras*. He reveals in the book that in all of France there were only fifty qualified reconnaissance crews, of which twenty-three were in his own unit. Within the first few days of the German onslaught in May of 1940, seventeen of the II/33 crews were sacrificed recklessly, he writes, "like glasses of water thrown onto a forest fire."

Saint-Exupéry survived the defeat, but was unimpressed with de Gaulle and refused to join the Royal Air Force as many of his contemporaries did. Instead, in late 1940, at the invitation of his American publishers, he came to New York to accept the National Book Award for *Wind, Sand and Stars*. He remained in the United States for more than two years, where he lived among French compatriots-in-exile and wrote *Flight to Arras*, *The Little Prince*, and *Letter to a Hostage*.

In the spring of 1943, a second long and fateful campaign to return to combat succeeded and, carrying a uniform supplied by a costumer for the Metropolitan Opera, he departed for North Africa to rejoin his old squadron. Then in July 1944, "risking flesh to prove good faith," he failed to return from a reconnaissance mission over his beloved France. At the time of his disappearance, Saint-Exupéry had just turned forty-four, and was at the height of the powers that are conveyed so movingly in *Flight to Arras*.

Walter J. Boyne

This volume, like every book in Wings of War, has been reproduced photographically from an original edition. It thus preserves the authenticity of the original, including typographical errors and printing irregularities.

Flight to Arras

By the author of

NIGHT FLIGHT

WIND, SAND AND STARS

Flight To Arras

by

Antoine de Saint=Exupéry

Translated from the French by
Lewis Galantière

Illustrated by Bernard Lamotte

Reynal & Hitchcock

New York

PRINTED IN THE UNITED STATES OF AMERICA BY
THE CORNWALL PRESS, INC., CORNWALL, NEW YORK

Flight to Arras

I

SURELY I must be dreaming. It is as if I were fifteen
again. I am back at school. My mind is on my
geometry problem. Leaning over the worn black
desk, I work away dutifully with compass and ruler and
protractor. I am quiet and industrious.

Near by sit some of my schoolmates, talking in
murmurs. One of them stands at a blackboard chalking
up figures. Others less studious are playing bridge. Out-
of-doors I see the branch of a tree swaying in the breeze.
I drop my work and stare at it. From an industrious
pupil I have become an idle one. The shining sun fills
me with peace. I inhale with delight the childhood odor
of the wooden desk, the chalk, the blackboard in this
schoolhouse in which we are quartered. I revel in the
sense of security born of this daydream of a sheltered
childhood.

What course life takes, we all know. We are children, we are sent to school, we make friends, we go to college—and we are graduated. Some sort of diploma is handed to us, and our hearts pound as we are ushered across a certain threshold, marched through a certain porch, the other side of which we are of a sudden grown men. Now our footfalls strike the ground with a new assurance. We have begun to make our way in life, to take the first few steps of our way in life. We are about to measure our strength against real adversaries. The ruler, the T square, the compass have become weapons with which we shall build a world, triumph over an enemy. Playtime is over.

All this I see as I stare at the swaying branch. And I see too that schoolboys have no fear of facing life. They champ at the bit. The jealousies, the trials, the sorrows of the life of man do not intimidate the schoolboy.

But what a strange schoolboy I am! I sit in this schoolroom, a schoolboy conscious of my good fortune and in no hurry to face life. A schoolboy aware of its cares. . . .

Dutertre comes by, and I stop him.

"Sit down. I'll do some card-tricks for you."

Dutertre sits facing me on a desk as worn as mine. I can see his dangling legs as he shuffles the cards. How pleased with myself I am when I pick out the card he has in mind! He laughs. Modestly, I smile. Pénicot comes up and puts his arm across my shoulder.

"What do you say, old boy?"

How tenderly peaceful all this is!

A school usher—is it an usher?—opens the door and summons two among us. They drop their ruler, drop their compass, get up, and go out. We follow them with our eyes. Their schooldays are over. They have been released for the business of life. What they have learnt, they are now to make use of. Like grown men, they are about to try out against other men the formulas they have worked out.

Strange school, this, where each goes forth alone in turn. And without a word of farewell. Those two who have just gone through the door did not so much as glance at us who remain behind. And yet the hazard of life, it may be, will transport them farther away than China. So much farther! When schooldays are past, and life has scattered you, who can swear that you will meet again?

The rest of us, those still nestling in the cosy warmth of our incubator, go back to our murmured talk.

"Look here, Dutertre. To-night—."

But once again the same door has opened. And like a court sentence the words ring out in the quiet schoolroom:

"Captain de Saint-Exupéry and Lieutenant Dutertre report to the major!"

Schooldays are over. Life has begun.

"Did you know it was our turn?"

"Pénicot flew this morning."

"Oh, yes."

The fact that we had been sent for meant that we were to be ordered out on a sortie. We had reached the last days of May, 1940, a time of full retreat, of full disaster. Crew after crew was being offered up as a sacrifice. It was as if you dashed glassfuls of water into a forest fire in the hope of putting it out. The last thing that could occur to any one in this world that was tumbling round our ears was the notion of risk or danger. Fifty reconnaissance crews was all we had for the whole French army. Fifty crews of three men each—pilot, observer, and gunner. Out of the fifty, twenty-three made up our unit—Group 2-33. In three weeks, seventeen of the twenty-three had vanished. Our Group had melted like a lump of wax. Yesterday, speaking to Lieutenant Gavoille, I had let drop the words, "Oh, we'll see about that when the war is over." And Gavoille had answered, "I hope you don't mean, Captain, that you expect to come out of the war alive?"

Gavoille was not joking. He was sincerely shocked. We knew perfectly well that there was nothing for us but to go on flinging ourselves into the forest fire. Even though it serve no purpose. Fifty crews for the whole of France. The whole strategy of the French army rested upon our shoulders. An immense forest fire raging, and a hope that it might be put out by the sacrifice of a few glassfuls of water. They would be sacrificed.

And this was as it should be. Who ever thought of complaining? When did anyone ever hear, among us, anything else than "Very good, sir. Yes, sir. Thank you, sir. Quite right, sir." Throughout the closing days of the French campaign one impression dominated all others—an impression of absurdity. Everything was cracking up all round us. Everything was caving in. The collapse was so entire that death itself seemed to us absurd. Death, in such a tumult, had ceased to count. But we ourselves did not count.

Dutertre and I went into the major's office. The major's name was Alias. As I write, he is still in command of Group 2-33, at Tunis.

"Afternoon, Saint-Ex. Hello, Dutertre. Sit down."

We sat down. The major spread out a map on the table and turned to his clerk:

"Fetch me the weather reports."

He sat tapping on the table with his pencil. I stared at him. His face was drawn. He had had no sleep. Back and forth in a motorcar, he had driven all night in search of a phantom General Staff. He had been summoned to division headquarters. To brigade headquarters. He had argued and wrangled with supply depots that never delivered the spare parts they promised. His car had been bottled up in the crazy traffic. He had supervised our last moving out and our most recent moving in—for we were driven by the enemy from one field to another like poor devils scrambling in the van of a relentless bailiff. Alias had succeeded in saving our planes, saving our lorries, saving the stores and files of the Group. He looked as if he had reached the end of his strength, of his nerves.

"Well," he said, and he went on tapping with his pencil. He was still not looking at us.

A moment passed before he spoke again. "It's damned awkward," he said finally; and he shrugged his shoulders. "A damned awkward sortie. But the Staff want it done. They very much want it done. I argued with them; but they want it done. . . . And that's that."

Dutertre and I sat looking out of the window. Here too a branch was swaying in the breeze. I could hear the cackle of the hens. Our Intelligence Room had been set up in a schoolhouse; the major's office was in a farmhouse.

It would be easy to write a couple of fraudulent pages out of the contrast between this shining spring day, the ripening fruit, the chicks filling plumply out in the barnyard, the rising wheat—and death at our elbow. I shall not write that couple of pages because I see no reason why the peace of a spring day should constitute a contradiction of the idea of death. Why should the sweetness of life be a matter for irony?

But a vague notion did go through my mind as I stared out of Alias' window. "The spring has broken down," I said to myself. "The season is out of order." I had flown over abandoned threshing machines, abandoned binders. I had seen motorcars deserted in roadside ditches. I had come upon a village square standing under water while the village faucet—"the fountain" as our people call it—stood open and the stream flowed on.

And suddenly a completely ridiculous image came into my mind. I thought of clocks out of order. All the clocks of France—out of order. Clocks in their church steeples. Clocks on railway stations. Chimney clocks in empty houses. A charnelhouse of clocks. "The war," I said to myself, "is that thing in which clocks are no longer wound up. In which beets are no longer gathered in. In which farm carts are no longer greased. And that water, collected and piped to quench men's thirst and to whiten the Sunday laces of the village women—that water stands now in a pool flooding the square before the village church."

As for Alias, he was talking like a bedside physician. "Hm," says the doctor with a shake of the head, "rather awkward, this"; and you know that he is hinting that you ought to be making your will, thinking of those you are about to leave behind. There was no question in Dutertre's mind or mine that Alias was talking about sacrificing another crew.

"And," Alias went on, "things being as they are, it's no good worrying about the chances you run."

Quite so. No good at all. And it's no one's fault. It's not our fault that we feel none too cheerful. Not the major's fault that he is ill at ease with us. Not the Staff's fault that it gives orders. The major is out of sorts because the orders are absurd. We know that they are absurd; but the Staff knows that as well as we do. It gives orders because orders have to be given. Giving orders is its trade, in time of war. And everyone knows what war looks like. Handsome horsemen transmit the orders—or rather, to be modern about it, motorcyclists. The orders ordain events, change the face of the world. The handsome horsemen are like the stars—they bring tidings of the future. In the midst of turmoil and despair, orders arrive, flung to the troops from the backs of steaming horses. And then all is well—at least, so says the blueprint of war. So says the pretty picture-book of war. Everybody struggles as hard as he can to make war look like war. Piously respects the rules of the game. So that war may perhaps be good enough to agree to look like war.

Orders are given for the sacrifice of the air arm because war must be made to look like war. And nobody admits meanwhile that this war looks like nothing at all. That no part of it makes sense. That not a single blueprint fits the circumstances. That the puppets have been cut free of the strings which continue to be pulled.

In all seriousness the Staffs issue orders that never reach anybody. They ask us for intelligence impossible to provide. But the air arm cannot undertake to explain war to the Staffs. Reconnaissance pilots might be able to test or verify the Staffs' hypotheses. But there are no longer any hypotheses. Fifty reconnaissance crews are asked to sketch the face of a war that has no face. The Staffs appeal to us as if we were a tribe of fortune-tellers.

While Alias was speaking I threw a glance at Dutertre—my fortune-telling observer. This was what he said afterwards.

"What do they take us for, sending us off on low-altitude sorties? Only yesterday I had to tick off a colonel from division headquarters who was talking the same rot. 'Will you tell me,' I said to him; 'will you tell me how I am going to report the enemy's position to you from an altitude of fifty feet when I'm doing three hundred miles an hour?' He looked at me as if I was the one who was mad. 'Why,' he said, 'that's easy. You can tell according to whether they shoot or not. If they shoot at you, the positions are German.' Imagine! The bloody fool!"

What Dutertre knew, and the colonel seemed to forget, was that the French army never saw French aeroplanes. We had roughly one thousand planes scattered between Dunkerque and Alsace. Diluted in infinity, so far as the men on the ground were concerned. The result was that when a plane roared across our lines, it was virtually certain to be a German. You let fly with all the anti-aircraft guns you had even before you saw him, the instant you heard him; for otherwise he had dropped his bombs and was off before you could say "wink!".

"A precious lot of intelligence we'll bring home working their way!" Dutertre said.

Of course they take our intelligence into account, since the blueprint of war requires that intelligence officers make use of intelligence. But even their war-by-the-blueprint had broken down. We knew perfectly well that they would never be able to make use of our intelligence—luckily. It might be brought back by us; but it would never be transmitted to the Staff. The roads would be jammed. The telephone lines would be cut. The Staff would have moved in a hurry. The really important intelligence—the enemy's position—would have been furnished by the enemy himself.

For example. A few days earlier we of Group 2-33, having been driven back by successive stages to the vicinity of Laon, were wondering how near the front might now be—how soon we should be forced to move again. A lieutenant was sent off for information to the general in command who was seven miles away. Halfway between the airfield and the general's headquarters the lieutenant's motorcar ran up against a steam-roller behind which two armored cars were hidden. The lieutenant made a U-turn and started away, but a blast of machine-gun fire killed him instantly and wounded his chauffeur. The armored cars were German. They taught us where the "front" was.

The General Staff was like a first-rate bridge player who is asked by someone sitting in a game in the next room, "What do you think I ought to do with the queen of spades?" How can the expert, knowing nothing of that particular game, have an opinion about that queen of spades?

Actually, a General Staff has no right to be without an opinion. Besides, so long as certain elements are still in its hands, it is bound to make use of them—since otherwise it will lose its control over them. The opponents will work a squeeze play. Thus, the General Staff must take risks. So long as there is a war on it must act, even though it act blindly.

But it is, nevertheless, very hard to say what shall be done with the queen of spades when you haven't a hand in the game. What we had learnt, meanwhile—at first with surprise, and then with the feeling that we ought to have seen it coming—was that once the cracking up begins, the machine stops running. There is no soldiering for the soldier to do.

You might think that in retreat and disaster there ought to be such a flood of pressing problems that one could hardly decide which to tackle first. The truth is that for a defeated army the problems themselves vanish. I mean by this that a defeated army no longer has a hand in the game. What is one to do with a plane, a tank, in short a queen of spades, that is not part of any known game? You hold the card back; you hesitate; you rack your brains to find use for it—and then you fling it down on the chance that it may take a trick.

Commonly, people believe that defeat is characterized by a general bustle and a feverish rush. Bustle and rush are the signs of victory, not of defeat. Victory is a thing of action. It is a house in the act of being built. Every participant in victory sweats and puffs, carrying the stones for the building of the house. But defeat is a thing of weariness, of incoherence, of boredom. And above all of futility.

For in the first place these sorties on which we were sent off were futile. More murderous and more futile with every day that passed. Against the avalanche that was overwhelming them our generals could defend themselves only with what they had. They had to fling down their trumps; and Dutertre and I, as we sat listening to the major, were their trumps.

The major was sketching for us the afternoon's program. He was sending us off to fly a photography sortie at thirty thousand feet and thereafter to do a reconnaissance job at two thousand feet above the German tank parks scattered over a considerable area round Arras. His voice was as deliberate as if he were saying, "and then you take the second street on the right to a square where you will see a tobacco shop."

What could we answer but "Very good, sir"? The sortie was as futile as that—the language as lyrical as the futility of the sortie required.

I had my own thoughts. "Another crew flung away," I said to myself. My head was buzzing, buzzing with many things; but I said to myself that I'd wait. If we got back, if we were alive that night, I'd do my thinking then.

If we were alive. When a sortie was not "awkward," one plane out of three got back. Naturally, the ratio was not the same when the sortie was a nasty one.

But I was not weighing my chances of getting back. Sitting there in the major's office, death seemed to me neither august, nor majestic, nor heroic, nor poignant. Death seemed to me a mere sign of disorder. A consequence of disorder. The Group was to lose us more or less as baggage becomes lost in the hubbub of changing trains.

Not that on the subject of war, of death, of sacrifice, of France I do not think quite other things than what I now say; but sitting in that office my thoughts were without a compass, my language was a blur. I sat thinking in contradictions. My concept of truth had been shattered, and the best I could do was to stare at one fragment after another. "If I am alive," I said to myself, "I shall do my thinking tonight." Night, the beloved. Night, when words fade and things come alive. When the destructive analysis of day is done, and all that is truly important becomes whole and sound again. When man reassembles his fragmentary self and grows with the calm of a tree.

Day belongs to family quarrels, but with the night he who has quarrelled finds love again. For love is greater than any wind of words. And man, leaning at his window under the stars, is once again responsible for the bread of the day to come, for the slumber of the wife who lies by his side, all fragile and delicate and contingent. Love is not thinking, but being. As I sat facing Alias I longed for night and for the rebirth in me of the being that merits love. For night, when my thoughts would be of civilization, of the destiny of man, of the savor of friendship in my native land. For night, so that I might yearn to serve some overwhelming purpose which at this moment I cannot define. For night, so that I might perhaps advance a step towards fixing it in my unmanageable language. I longed for night as the poet might do, the true poet who feels himself inhabited by a thing obscure but powerful, and who strives to erect images like ramparts round that thing in order to capture it. To capture it in a snare of images.

And as I sat there longing for night, I was for the moment like a Christian abandoned by grace. I was about to do my job with Dutertre honorably, that was certain. But to do it as one honors ancient rites when they have no longer any significance. When the god that lived in them has withdrawn from them. I should wait for night, I said to myself; and if I was still alive I would walk alone on the highway that runs through our village. Alone and safely isolated in my beloved solitude. So that I might discover why it is I ought to die.

II

I AWOKE out of my daydream—was startled out of it by an astonishing proposal.

"If this sortie bothers you, Saint-Ex; if you don't feel up to it today, I can—."

"Oh, come, Major!"

He knew perfectly well that his proposal was idiotic. And I knew why he made it. If a pilot doesn't get back you begin to recall how solemn he was when he was ordered out. You say to yourself that he must have had a premonition of his end. And you accuse yourself of having wilfully brushed it aside. You take time out for an attack of conscience.

The major's scruple reminded me of Israel. Two days before, I had been sitting smoking at the window of the Intelligence Room. Israel, when I caught sight of him through the window, was walking swiftly past. His nose was red. A big nose, very Jewish and very red. Suddenly there had seemed to me something queer about that big red nose.

This Israel, whose nose I was staring at, was a man I profoundly liked. He was one of the most courageous pilots of the Group. One of the most courageous and one of the most modest. He had heard so much talk of Jewish craftiness that he probably mistook his courage for a form of craftiness. To gain a victory is to act craftily.

There I sat, watching that red nose that gleamed in my sight only for an instant, so swift were the steps that carried Israel and his nose out of view. I turned to Gavoille, and without meaning to make a joke of it, I said:

"Why do you suppose his nose is like that?"

Gavoille answered: "His mother made it like that." And then added quickly: "Low-altitude sortie. Can't blame the fellow."

That night, when we had given up looking for Israel to get back, I thought again of that nose, planted in the middle of a totally expressionless face and yet revealing, with a sort of genius of its own, the burden of the thoughts revolving in the man's mind. If it had been my job to order Israel on that sortie, the memory of his nose would have haunted me like a reproach. Israel, surely, had responded to the order with no more than a "Yes, sir," a "Very good, sir." Israel, surely, had not allowed a single muscle of his face to quiver on hearing the order. But gently, insidiously, treacherously, his nose had reddened. Israel had been able to control the muscles of his face, but not the color of his nose. And in the silence in which he had received the order, his nose had taken advantage of him. Unknown to Israel, it had made clear to the major its emphatic disapproval of the sortie.

This was the kind of thing that made Alias hesitate to send into action men he imagined might be subject to premonitions. Premonitions are more often false than true; but when you are seized by one, a military order will sound like a court sentence. And Alias was not a judge, after all, but a group commander.

There was the case the other day of the gunner I shall call T. As Israel was all courage, so T. was all fear. He is the only man I have ever known who really felt fear. When, during the war, you gave T. an order you released in him at that moment a wave of dizziness. Something simple, relentless, and gradual. Rising slowly from his feet to his head, a stiffening would come over his whole body. Little by little his face would go totally blank. And his eyes would begin to shine.

Unlike Israel, whose nose, reddened with irritation, had seemed to me so dejected at the thought of the probable death of Israel, no psychic mutation took place in T. He did not react, he moulted. When you had finished giving T. an order you discovered that you had lit a flame of anguish in him, and that the anguish had begun to spread a sort of even glow through his being. Thereafter, nothing at all could reach him. You felt in the man the gradual spread of a desert of indifference that intervened between him and the universe. Never in any

other man on earth have I perceived this form of ec-
stacy.

"I shouldn't have let him fly that day," Alias said to
me later. For that day, when the major had given T. his
orders, T. had not merely turned white, he had begun
to smile. Quite plainly to smile. Probably as tortured
men smile when, really, the executioner has gone too
far.

"You're off your feed today, T. I'll get another gunner."

"If you please, sir. It's my turn," T. had answered.
He was standing respectfully at attention, eyes front
and perfectly motionless.

"Still, if you don't feel sure of yourself—."

"It's my turn out, sir."

"Come, T., look here—."

"Sir!" T. had interrupted; and his whole body looked
carved out of rock.

"So," Alias concluded, "I let him have his way."

Exactly what happened, we never knew. T., sitting
aft as gunner of the crew, had seen a German fighter
bear down on him. The German's guns had jammed,
and he had turned tail and vanished. T. had exchanged
remarks with his pilot through the speaking tube all the
way back to the neighborhood of their base. The pilot
had observed nothing abnormal in T.'s conversation.
But about five minutes before landing T. had stopped
talking, and the pilot had been unable to raise him.

That same evening, T. was brought in, his skull split

open by the tail-unit of his own plane. He had tried to bail out over home territory where he was completely out of danger. The plane had been flying at high speed, and he had done a bad job of parachuting. The passage of that German fighter had been irresistible, a siren call.

"Better get along and dress, now," the major said. "I want you off the ground at five-thirty."

We said, "See you this evening, sir," and the major responded by a vague wave of the hand. Was it superstition? I turned to leave, became aware that my cigarette was out, and was fumbling in vain through all my pockets when the major said testily:

"Why is it you never carry any matches?"

It was true; and with this substitute for "Good luck!" in my ears I shut the door saying to myself, "Why is it I never have a match on me?"

Dutertre said, "This sortie has got on his nerves."

He doesn't give a damn about it, I thought. But I didn't say so aloud, for I wasn't thinking of Alias. I was thinking of man in general. I had been brought up with a jerk by a very evident fact which men do not trouble to see—that the life of the spirit, the veritable life, is intermittent, and only the life of the mind is constant. This instant and spontaneous reflection leads back to Alias in a roundabout way.

Man's spirit is not concerned with objects; that is the business of our analytical faculties. Man's spirit is concerned with the significance that relates objects to one another. With their totality, which only the piercing eye of the spirit can perceive. The spirit, meanwhile, alternates between total vision and absolute blindness. Here is a man, for example, who loves his farm—but there are moments when he sees in it only a collection of unrelated objects. Here is a man who loves his wife—but there are moments when he sees in love nothing but burdens, hindrances, constraints. Here is a man who loves music—but there are moments when it cannot reach him. What we call a nation is certainly not the sum of the regions, customs, cities, farms, and the rest that man's intelligence is able at any moment to add up. It is a Being. But there are moments when I find myself blind to beings—even to the being called France.

Major Alias had spent the previous night at Staff headquarters discussing what was in effect pure logic. Pure logic is the ruin of the spirit. Afterwards he had driven back, and driving back he had worn himself out getting through the tangled traffic. Having finally reached his billet he had found a hundred details to look after, those details that fray a man's nerves and set him on edge. And this afternoon he had sent for us and ordered us to embark upon an utterly impossible sortie. What were we to him? Particles in the universal chaos. We were not Saint-Exupéry and Dutertre to him—each with our own way of seeing or not seeing things, of thinking, walking, smiling, drinking. We were mere details in a vast structure to see the whole of which demanded more time, more silence, more perspective than

he could possibly obtain. Had my face been afflicted
with a tic, he would have been able to see nothing but
the tic. He would have sent out over Arras the memory
of a tic. In this senseless hullabaloo, in this avalanche, we
ourselves, each of us, saw nothing but particles. That
voice. That nose. That tic. And particles are not the objects of anybody's emotion.

Thus I was not thinking about Alias specifically, but
about man in general. A friend you love has died, and it
is you who must see that he is decently buried. At that
moment you have no contact with your dead friend.
How can you have? Death is a thing of grandeur. It
brings instantly into being a whole new network of relations between you and the ideas, the desires, the habits of the man now dead. It is a rearrangement of the
world. Nothing has changed visibly, yet everything has
changed. The pages of the book are the same, but the
meaning of the book is different. And how can you,
who are busy with funeral details, know any of this?
Do you wish to bring the dead friend to mind? You
must be able to imagine yourself needing him. At that
moment you will miss him. Imagine him needing
you. Ah, but he no longer needs you! Imagine those
Wednesdays when, invariably, you lunched together.
Wednesday is now a vacuum. Life, we know, has to be
seen in perspective. But on a day of burial there is no
perspective—for space itself is annihilated. Your dead
friend is still a fragmentary being. The day you bury
him is a day of chores and crowds, of hands false or true

to be shaken, of the immediate cares of mourning. The
dead friend will not really die until tomorrow, when
silence is round you again. Then he will show himself
complete, as he was—to tear himself away, as he was,
from the substantial you. Only then will you cry out
because of him who is leaving and whom you cannot
detain.

I am still on the track of my thought when I say that
I do not like the pretty picture-book of war. The gruff
warrior squeezing back a tear and hiding his honest emotion under a grumpy exterior. What nonsense! The
gruff warrior is not hiding anything at all. If he lets fly
a gruff remark it is because a gruff remark has come into
his mind.

Nor does it matter for my purpose whether a man be
decent or a brute. Major Alias is a sensitive person. If
Dutertre and I fail to get back it will probably affect
him more than anyone else in the Group. Provided,
however, that he think of Saint-Exupéry and Dutertre,
and not of a sum of unrelated particles. Provided that he
be allowed the silence in which to effect this reconstruc-
tion of ourselves. For if, tonight, the bailiff at our heels
once more constrains the Group to move, a single
broken-down lorry will suffice to put off our death until another time. Alias will forget to be affected by our
death.

The life of the spirit, I say, is intermittent. My own
spirit as much as Alias'. I am off on an "awkward" sortie.
Is my mind filled with the thought of the war of the

Nazi against the Occident? Not at all. I think in terms of immediate details. I think of possible wounds. I think of the absurdity of flying over German-held Arras at two thousand feet. Of the futility of the intelligence we are asked to bring back. Of the interminable time it takes to dress in these clothes that remind me of men made ready for the executioner. And I think of my gloves. Where the devil are my gloves? I have lost my gloves.

I can no longer see the cathedral in which I live. I am dressing for the service of a dead god.

" *. . . and then you take the second street on the right.*" (PAGE 22)

III

"GET going! Where are my gloves? . . . No, not those. Have a look in my bag."

"Sorry, sir. Can't find them."

"God, you're a fool!"

Everybody is a fool. My orderly, who doesn't know where my gloves are. Hitler, who unloosed this mad war. And that fellow on the General Staff, obsessed by low-altitude sorties.

"I asked you to get me a pencil. I have been asking you for ten minutes to find me a pencil. Haven't you got a pencil?"

"Here it is, sir."

One man, at least, who is not a fool.

"Tie a string round it. Now knot the string through this buttonhole. . . . I say, gunner, you seem to be taking things very easily."

"I'm all ready, sir."

37

"Oh!"

And my observer. I swung round to him.

"Everything shipshape, Dutertre? Nothing missing? Worked out your course?"

He has worked out his course. "Awkward" sortie indeed! Where is the sense, I ask you, in sending a crew out to be murdered for the sake of intelligence that is sure to be useless and will never reach the Staff anyway, even if one of us lives to report it?

"Mediums," I said aloud. "They must have a crew of mediums on the General Staff."

"What do you mean, Captain?"

"How do *you* think we'll report to them? They are going to communicate with us. Table tipping. Automatic writing."

Not very funny; but I went on grousing.

"General Staffs! Let them fly their own damned sorties!"

It takes a long time to dress for a sortie that you know is a hopeless one. A long time to harness yourself only for the fun of being blasted to bits. There are three thicknesses of clothing to be put on, one over the other: that takes time. And this clutter of accessories that you carry about like an itinerant pedlar! All this complication of oxygen tubes, heating equipment; these speaking tubes that form the "inter-com" running between the members of the crew. This mask through which I breathe. I am attached to the plane by a rubber tube as indispensable as an umbilical cord. The plane is plugged in to the circulation of my blood. Organs have been added to my being, and they seem to intervene between me and my heart. From one minute to the next I grow heavier, more cumbrous, harder to handle. I turn round all of a piece, and when I bend down to tighten my straps or pull at buckles that resist, all my joints creak aloud. My old fractures begin to hurt again.

"Hand me another helmet. I've told you twenty times that my own won't do. It's too tight."

God knows why, but a man's skull swells at high altitude. A helmet that fits perfectly on the ground becomes a vise pressing on the skull at thirty thousand feet.

"But this is another helmet, sir. I sent back your old one."

"Huh!"

I cannot stop grousing, and I grouse without remorse. A lot of good it does! Not that it is important. This is the moment of timelessness. This is the crossing of the inner desert of anguish. There is no god here. There is no face to love. There is no France, no Europe, no civilization. There are particles, detritus, nothing more. I feel no shame at this moment in praying for a miracle that should change the course of this afternoon. The miracle, for instance, of a speaking tube out of order. Speaking tubes are always going out of order. Trashy stuff! A speaking tube out of order would preserve us from the holocaust.

Captain Vezin came in with a gloomy look. No pilot ever got off the ground without a dose of Captain Vezin's gloom. His job was to report upon the position of the Germain air outposts. To tell us where they were. Vezin is my friend and I am very fond of him; but he is a bird of ill omen. I prefer not to meet him when I am about to take off.

"Looks bad, old boy," said Vezin. "Very bad. Very bad indeed."

And didn't he pull a sheaf of papers out of his pocket, to impress me! Then, looking at me suspiciously, he said:

"How are you going out?"

"By the town of Albert."

"I thought so. I knew it. Bad business."

"Stop talking like a bloody fool! What's up?"

"You'll never make it. You'll have to give up this sortie."

Give up this sortie! Very kind of him to say so. Let him tell that to God the Father. Perhaps He'll put a curse on our speaking tubes.

"You'll never get through, I tell you."

"And why will I never get through?"

"Because there are three groups of German fighters circling permanently over Albert. One at eighteen thousand feet, another at twenty-five thousand, and a third at thirty-three thousand. They fly in relays and hang on until they are relieved. It's what I call *categorically blocked*. You'll fly straight into a German net. See here. . . ."

He shoved a sheet of paper at me on which he had scribbled an absolutely unintelligible demonstration of his argument.

Vezin had done much better to keep his nose out of my affairs. His pompous *categorically blocked* had impressed me, confound him! I thought instantly of red lights and traffic tickets. Only, this was a place where a ticket meant death. It was his *categorically* that particularly galled me. It seemed to be aimed at me personally.

I made a great effort to think clearly. "The enemy," I said to myself, "always defends his position *categorically*. Damned nonsense, these big words! And besides, why should I worry about German fighter planes? At thirty thousand feet they would get me before I so much as suspected their presence, and at two thousand feet it was the anti-aircraft that would bring me down, not the fighters. It couldn't possibly miss me." Suddenly I became belligerent.

"In short, what you're telling me is that the Germans have an air force, and therefore my sortie is not altogether advisable. Run along and tell that to the general."

It wouldn't have cost Vezin anything to reassure me pleasantly, instead of upsetting me. Why couldn't he have said, "Oh, by the way. The Germans have a few fighters aloft over Albert"?

It would have come to the same thing.

We climbed in. I had still to test the inter-com.

"Can you hear me, Dutertre?"

"I hear you, Captain."

"You, gunner! Hear me?"

"I . . . Yes, sir. Clearly."

"Dutertre! Can you hear the gunner?"

"Clearly, Captain."

"Gunner! Can you hear Lieutenant Dutertre?"

"I . . . er . . . Yes, sir. Clearly."

"What makes you stutter back there? What are you hesitating about?"

"Sorry, sir. I was looking for my pencil."

The speaking tubes were not out of order.

"Gunner! Have a look at your oxygen bottles. Air-pressure normal?"

"I . . . Yes, sir. Normal."

"In all three bottles?"

"All three, sir."

"All set, Dutertre?"

"All set, Captain."

"All set, gunner?"

"All set, sir."

We took off.

IV

HUMAN anguish is the product of the loss by man of his true identity. I sit waiting for a telegram which is to announce to me either a death or a recovery. Time flows by unutilized and holds me in suspense. Time has ceased to be a stream that feeds me, nourishes me, adds growth to me as to a tree. The man that I shall be when the news comes, dwells outside me: he is moving towards me like a ghost about to fuse with me. And for want of knowing who I am, I am suspended in anguish. The bad news, when it comes, puts an end to my suspense. It causes me to suffer, which is not the same thing.

T. never knew whether, in the hour to come, he was to be transmuted into a living man or a dead man. He was aware of only one thing—the flow of time, running like sand through his fingers while he waited for the coming of a certain instant too rich in power for his resistance.

For me, piloting my plane, time has ceased to run sterile through my fingers. Now, finally, I am installed in my function. Time is no longer a thing apart from me. I have stopped projecting myself into the future. I am no longer he who may perhaps dive down the sky in a vortex of flame. The future is no longer a haunting phantom, for from this moment on I shall myself create the future by my own successive acts. I am he who checks the course and holds the compass at 313°. Who controls the revolutions of the propeller and the temperature of the oil. These are healthy and immediate cares. These are household cares, the little duties of the day that take away the sense of growing older. The day becomes a house brilliantly clean, a floor well waxed, oxygen prudently doled out. . . . Thinking which, I check the oxygen flow, for we have been rising fast and are at twenty-two thousand feet already.

"Oxygen all right, Dutertre? How do you feel?"

"First rate, Captain."

"You, gunner! How's your oxygen?"

"I . . . er . . . Shipshape, sir."

"Haven't you found that pencil yet?"

And I am he who checks his machine guns, putting a finger on button S, on button A. . . . Which reminds me.

"Gunner! No good-sized town behind you, in your cone of fire?"

"Er . . . all clear, sir."

"Check your guns. Let fly."

I hear the blast of the guns.

"Work all right?"

"Worked fine, sir."

"All of them?"

"Er . . . yes, sir. All of them."

I test my own and wonder what becomes of all the bullets that we scatter so heedlessly over our home territory. They never kill any one. The earth is vast.

Now time is nourishing me with every minute that passes. I am a thing as little the prey of anguish as a ripening fruit. Of course the circumstances of this flight will change round me. The circumstances and the problems. But I dwell now well inside the fabrication of the future. Time, little by little, is kneading me into shape. A child is not frightened at the thought of being patiently transmuted into an old man. He is a child and he plays like a child. I too play my games. I count the dials, the levers, the buttons, the knobs of my kingdom. I count one hundred and three objects to check, pull, turn, or press. (Perhaps I have cheated in counting my machine-gun controls as two—one for the fire-button, and another for the safety-catch.) Tonight when I get back I shall amaze the farmer with whom I am billeted. I shall say to him:

"Do you know how many instruments a pilot has to keep his eye on?"

"How do you expect me to know that?"

"No matter. Guess. Name a figure."

"What figure?"

My farmer is not a man of tact.

"Any figure. Name one."

"Seven."

"One hundred and three!"

And I shall smile with satisfaction.

Another thing contributes to my peace of mind—it is that all the instruments that were an encumbrance while I was dressing have now settled into place and acquired meaning. All that tangle of tubes and wiring has become a circulatory network. I am an organism integrated into the plane. I turn this switch, which gradually heats up my overall and my oxygen, and the plane begins to generate my comfort. The oxygen, incidentally, is too hot. It burns my nose. A complicated mechanism releases it in proportion to the altitude at which I fly, and I am flying high. The plane is my wet-nurse. Before we took off, this thought seemed to me inhuman; but now, suckled by the plane itself, I feel a sort of filial affection for it. The affection of a nursling.

My weight, meanwhile, is comfortably distributed over a variety of points of support. I am like a feeble convalescent stripped of bodily consciousness and lying in a chaise-longue. The convalescent exists only as a frail thought. My triple thickness of clothing is without weight in my seat. My parachute, slung behind, lies against the back of my seat. My enormous boots rest on the bar that operates the rudder. My hands that are so awkward when first I slip on the thick stiff gloves, handle the wheel with ease. Handle the wheel. Handle the wheel. . . .

"Dutertre!"

". . . t'n?"

"Something's wrong with the inter-com. I can't hear
you. Check your contacts."

"I can . . . you . . . ctly."

"Shake it up! Can you still hear me?"

Dutertre's voice came through clearly.

"Hear you perfectly, Captain."

"Good! Dutertre, the confounded controls are frozen
again. The wheel is stiff and the rudder is stuck fast."

"That's great! What altitude?"

"Thirty-two thousand."

"Temperature?"

"Fifty-five below zero. How's your oxygen?"

"Coming fine."

"Gunner! How's your oxygen?"

No answer.

"Hi! Gunner!"

No answer.

"Do you hear the gunner, Dutertre?"

"No."

"Call him."

"Gunner! Gunner!"

No answer.

"He must have passed out, Captain. We shall have to
dive."

I didn't want to dive unless I had to. The gunner
might have dropped off to sleep. I shook up the plane
as roughly as I could.

"Captain, sir?"

"That you, gunner?"

"I . . . er . . . yes, sir."

"Not sure it's you?"

"Yes, sir."

"Why the devil didn't you answer before?"

"I had pulled the plug, sir. I was testing the radio."

"You're a bloody fool! Do you think you're alone in this plane? I was just about to dive. I thought you were dead."

"Er . . .. no, sir."

"I'll take your word for it. But don't play that trick on me again. Damn it! Let me know before you cut."

"Sorry, sir. I will. I'll let you know, sir."

Had his oxygen flow stopped working, he wouldn't have known it. The human body receives no warning. A vague swooning comes over you. In a few seconds you have fainted. In a few minutes you are dead. The flow has constantly to be tested—particularly by the pilot. I pinched my tube lightly a few times and felt the warm life-bringing puffs blow round my nose.

It came to this, that I was working at my trade. All that I felt was the physical pleasure of going through gestures that meant something and were sufficient unto themselves. I was conscious neither of great danger (it had been different while I was dressing) nor of performing a great duty. At this moment the battle between the Nazi and the Occident was reduced to the scale of my job, of my manipulation of certain switches, levers, taps. This was as it should be. The sexton's love of his God becomes a love of lighting candles. The sexton moves with deliberate step through a church of which he is barely conscious, happy to see the candlesticks bloom one after the other as the result of his ministrations. When he has lighted them all, he rubs his hands. He is proud of himself.

I for my part am doing a good job of regulating the revolutions of the propeller, and the needle of my compass lies within a single degree of my course. If Dutertre happens to have his eye on the compass, he must be marvelling at me.

"I say, Dutertre! Compass on the course? How does it look?"

"Won't do, Captain. Too much drift. A little kick to starboard."

Well, well.

"Crossing our lines, Captain. I've started my camera. What's your altitude?"

"Thirty-three thousand."

V

"YOUR course, Captain!"

He's right. I was drifting to port. And not by chance, either. It was the town of Albert that was putting me off. I could make it faintly out, far ahead. But already it was shouldering me off with all the weight of its *categorically blocked*. Extraordinary, the memory secreted in the recesses of the human body. My body was remembering every sudden crash of the past, every cranial fracture, each of those nights in hospital with their comas as sticky as molasses. My body is afraid of blows. It struggles to avoid Albert. The moment I leave it to itself, we drift to port. It shies left like an old horse fearful for life of the obstacle that had once frightened it. And it is really my body, not my mind that I mean. The moment my mind wanders, my body takes sly advantage of me to slip around Albert.

For it is not I who feel any anxiety. I have stopped

wishing to get out of this sortie. On the ground, it had seemed to me that that was what I wanted. I had said to myself hopefully that the inter-com would be out of order. I was weary, and it would be wonderful to sleep. The bed of idleness had seemed to me a magic couch. But deep down I had known perfectly well that nothing could come of getting out of this sortie except a sharp sense of discomfort. As if a necessary moulting had miscarried.

Again I was reminded of school. Of a time when I was very young. How long ago was that? I—.

"Captain!"

"What's up?"

"Er . . . nothing. I thought I had seen something."

I don't like Dutertre seeing things. . . .

Of school, yes. When you are a little boy, in boarding school, they get you up too early. They get you up at six o'clock. It is cold. You rub your eyes, and you hate class long before the bell rings. You think how wonderful it would be if you were ill and were waking up in the infirmary, where the matron would be ready with a hot cup of camomile with lots of sugar in it. The infirmary becomes a kind of paradise in your mind.

I was like that; and naturally, the first time that I caught cold I coughed much more than was called for. And I awoke in the infirmary to the sound of the bell ringing for the others. But that bell punished me for cheating. It changed me into a wraith. It rang out the passing of living hours—hours of class with its austerity,

" . . . *this clutter of accessories that you carry about like an itinerant pedlar!*" (PAGE 38)

of play-time with its tumult, of the refectory with its warmth. For those who were alive, who were not, like me, in the infirmary, it sounded the realities of an enviable existence filled with jubilations, disappointments, severities, triumphs. And I lay robbed, forgotten, sick of insipid camomiles, of the sweaty bed, the blank hours.

Nothing comes of a sortie you have got out of.

Of course there are days like this when a sortie brings no satisfaction. It is too evident that we are playing a game that we call war. We are playing Cops and Robbers. We are abiding scrupulously by the rules of conduct prescribed by the history books and the rules of tactics prescribed by the war manuals. Last night, for example, I drove up to the aerodrome in a motorcar. The sentry, obedient to the rules, presented his bayonet. My car might as easily have been a German tank. We are playing at presenting bayonets to German tanks. But the tanks are playing their own game.

How can we possibly be enthusiastic about these grim charades, in which we play the part of supernumeraries, when we are asked to play on till we are killed? Death is a bit too serious for a charade. Who can dress with enthusiasm for such a part? Nobody . . . Even Hochedé who is a sort of saint, a man who has reached that state of permanent grace which surely is the final consummation of man—even Hochedé took refuge in silence. All of us dressed in silence, grumpily—and not because we were heroically modest. That grumpiness concealed no inner exaltation. It told its own story. And I knew what it meant. It was the grumpiness of an agent who is mystified by the instructions of an absentee owner, yet remains faithful to him. All of us longed for our quiet rooms, but there was not one who would really have chosen to go to bed.

For enthusiasm is not the important thing. There is no hope of enthusiasm in defeat. The important thing is to dress, climb aboard, and take off. What we ourselves think of the procedure is of no importance. A little boy in school enthusiastic about his grammar lesson would seem to me a little prig not to be trusted. The important thing is to strive towards a goal which is not immediately visible. That goal is not the concern of the mind, but of the spirit. The spirit knows how to love, but it is asleep. Talk to me about temptation! I know as much about temptation as any church father. To be tempted is to be tempted, when the spirit is asleep, to give in to the reasons of the mind.

What do I accomplish by risking my life in this mountain avalanche? I have no notion. Time and again people would say to me, "I can arrange to have you transferred here or there. That is where you belong. You will be more useful there than in a squadron. Pilots! We can train pilots by the thousand! Whereas you—." No question but that they were right. My mind agreed with them, but my instinct always prevailed over my mind.

Why was it that their reasoning never convinced me, even though I had no argument with which to defeat it? I would say to myself, "Intellectuals are kept in reserve on the shelves of the Propaganda Ministry, like pots of jam to be eaten when the war is over." Hardly an argument, I agree!

And now once again, like every other soldier of the Group, I have taken off in the face of every good reason, every obvious argument, every intellectual reflex. The moment will come when I shall know that it was reasonable to fight against reason. I have promised myself that if I am alive I shall walk alone on the highway that runs through our village. Then perhaps I shall dwell at last in my own self. And I shall see.

It may be that I shall have nothing to say about what I then see. When a woman seems to me beautiful, I have no words to say so. I see her smile, and that is all. Intellectuals take her face apart and explain it bit by bit. They do not see that smile.

To know is not to prove, nor to explain. It is to accede to vision. But if we are to have vision, we must learn to participate in the object of the vision. The apprenticeship is hard.

All day long my village was invisible to me. Before the sortie I saw in it nothing but mud walls and peasants more or less grimy. Now it is a handful of gravel thirty-three thousand feet below me. That is my village. But tonight, it may be, a watch dog will waken and bark. I have always loved the enchantment of a village dreaming aloud in the fair night by the voice of a single watch dog. And now what I ask is to see again my village tidied for sleep, its doors prudently shut upon its barns, its cattle, its customs. To see its peasants, home from the fields, their evening meal eaten and their table cleared, their children put to bed and their lamp blown out, dissolved into the silent night. And nothing more—unless perhaps, under the stiff white sheets of the countryside, the slow pulsation of their breathing, like the subsidence of a swell after a storm at sea.

God suspends the use of things and speech for the period of the nocturnal balance sheet. By the play of that irresistible slumber which loosens the fingers until morning, men will appear in my vision with open hands. And then perhaps I shall win a glimpse of that which has no name. I shall walk like the blind whose palms lead them towards the flame in the hearth. The blind cannot describe the flame, yet they have found it. Thus perhaps shall I see what it is in that dark village that we must die to protect—that which is unseen, yet like an ember beneath the ashes, lives on.

Nothing comes of a sortie you have got out of. If you are to understand a thing as simple as a village, you must first—.

"Captain!"

"Yes?"

"Six German fighters on the port bow."

The words rang in my ears like a thunderclap.

You must first. . . . You must first. . . . Ah! I do want very much to be paid off in time. I do want to have the right to love. I do want to win a glimpse of the being for whom I die.

VI

"GUNNER!"

"Sir?"

"D'you hear the lieutenant? Six German fighters. Six, on the port bow."

"I heard the lieutenant, sir."

"Dutertre! Have they seen us?"

"They have, Captain. Banking towards us. Fifteen hundred feet below us."

"Hear that, gunner? Fifteen hundred feet below us. Dutertre! How near are they?"

"Say ten seconds."

"Hear that, gunner? On our tail in a few seconds."

There they are. I see them. Tiny. A swarm of poisonous wasps.

"Gunner! They're crossing broadside. You'll see them in a second. There!"

"Don't see them yet, sir. . . . Yes, I do!"

I no longer see them myself.

"They after us?"

"After us, sir."

"Rising fast?"

"Can't say, sir. Don't think so. . . . No, sir."

Dutertre spoke. "What do you say, Captain?"

"What do you expect me to say?"

Nobody said anything. There was nothing to say. We were in God's hands. If I banked, I should narrow the space between us. Luckily, we were flying straight into the sun. At high altitude you cannot go up fifteen hundred feet higher without giving a couple of miles to your game. It was possible therefore that they might lose us entirely in the sun by the time they had reached our altitude and recovered their speed.

"Still after us, gunner?"

"Still after us, sir."

"We gaining on them?"

"Well, sir. No. . . . Perhaps."

It was God's business—and the sun's.

Fighters do not fight, they murder. Still, it might turn into a fight, and I made ready for it. I pressed with both feet as hard as I could, trying to free the frozen rudder. A wave of something strange went over me. But my eyes were still on the Germans, and I bore with all my weight down upon the rigid bar.

Once again I discovered that I was in fact much less upset in this moment of action—if "action" was the word for this vain expectancy—than I had been while dressing.

A kind of anger was going through me. A beneficent anger. God knows, no ecstasy of sacrifice. Rather an urge to bite hard into something.

"Gunner! Are we losing them?"

"We are losing them, sir."

Good job.

"Dutertre! Dutertre!"

"Captain?"

"I . . . nothing."

"Anything the matter?"

"Nothing. I thought. . . . Nothing."

I decided not to mention it..No good worrying them. If I went into a dive they would know it soon enough. They would know that I had gone into a dive.

It was not natural that I should be running with sweat in a temperature sixty degrees below zero. Not natural. I knew perfectly well what was happening. Gently, very gently, I was fainting.

I could see the instrument panel. Now I couldn't. My hands were losing their grip on the wheel. I hadn't even the strength to speak. I was letting myself go. So pleasant, letting oneself go. . . .

Then I squeezed the rubber tube. A gust of air blew into my nose and brought me life. The oxygen supply was not out of order! Then it must be. . . . Of course! How stupid I had been! It was the rudder. I had exerted myself like a man trying to pick up a grand piano. Flying thirty-three thousand feet in the air, I had struggled like a professional wrestler. The oxygen was being doled out to me. It was my business to use it up economically. I was paying for my orgy.

I began to inhale in swift repeated gasps. My heart beat faster and faster. It was like a faint tinkle. What good would it do to speak of it? If I went into a dive, they would know soon enough. Now I could see my instrument panel. . . . No, that wasn't true. I couldn't see it. Sitting there in my sweat, I was sad.

Life came back as gently as it had flowed out of me.

"Dutertre!"

"Captain?"

I should have liked to tell him what had happened.

"I . . . I thought . . . No."

I gave it up. Words consume oxygen too fast. Already I was out of breath. I was very weak. A convalescent.

"You were about to say something, Captain?"

"No. . . . Nothing."

"Quite sure, Captain? You puzzle me?"

I puzzle him. But I am alive.

"We are alive."

"Well, yes. For the time being."

For the time being. There was still Arras.

Thus for a minute or two I had the feeling that I should not pull through; and yet I had not observed in myself that poignant anxiety which, people say, turns the hair white in an instant. I began to think of Sagon, of what Sagon had said when, two months earlier, we had gone to see him only a few hours after he had been shot down behind our own lines. What had gone through his mind when the German fighters had surrounded him and nailed him to the stake.

VII

I SEE him exactly as he was, lying in the hospital bed. His knee had been hooked and broken by the tail-unit of the plane in the course of a parachute jump, but Sagon had not felt the shock. His face and hands were rather badly burnt, but all in all Sagon's condition was not alarming. Slowly and in a matter of fact voice, as if reporting a bit of fatigue duty, he told us his story.

"I knew they had got me when I saw the air filled with tracer bullets round my plane. My instrument panel was shot to bits. Then I saw a puff of smoke forward. It wasn't much, you know. I thought it must be . . . you know . . . there's a connecting pipe. There wasn't much flame."

He stopped, and his lower lip came forward while he turned it over in his mind. It seemed to him important to be able to tell us whether the flames were high or were not high. He hesitated: "But still, flame is flame. The inter-com was working, and I told the crew they'd better jump."

In less than ten seconds a plane can turn into a torch.

"Then I opened my escape hatch. I shouldn't have done that. It let in the air . . . and the flame, you know. . . . I was sorry I'd done it."

You have a locomotive boiler spitting a torrent of flame at you, twenty thousand feet in the air, and you are sorry you've done something. I shall not play Sagon false by talking of his heroism or his modesty. He would not recognize himself in these terms. He would insist that he was sorry he had done it. As we stood round his bed it was plain that he was making a concentrated effort to be precise.

The field of consciousness is tiny. It accepts only one problem at a time. Get into a fist fight, put your mind on the strategy of the fight, and you will not feel the other fellow's punches. Once, when I thought I was about to drown in a seaplane accident, the freezing water seemed to me tepid. Or, more exactly, my consciousness was not concerned with the temperature of the water. It was absorbed by other thoughts. The temperature of the water has left no trace in my memory. In the same way, Sagon's consciousness was filled to the brim with the problem of getting away from the plane. His universe was limited successively to the fate of his crew, the handle that governed the sliding hatch, the rip cord of the parachute.

The inter-com seemed to be working. "Are you there?" he had called out.

No answer.

"Nobody on board?" he had asked again.

No answer.

They must have jumped, Sagon had decided. And as he was sorry about those flames (his hands and face were already burnt), he had got out of his seat, climbed out on the fuselage, and crawled forward along the surface of the wing.

"I peered in. I couldn't see the observer."

The observer, killed instantly by the German fighters, had slumped down out of sight.

"Then I backed up and looked for the gunner. I couldn't see him, either."

But the same thing had happened to the gunner.

"I thought they must have jumped."

Once again Sagon turned the matter over in his mind.

"If I had known, I could have crawled back into the cockpit. The flames were not so high. I lay there on the wing, I don't know how long. I had stabilized the plane at an angle before crawling out. The going was smooth, the wind was bearable, and I felt fairly comfortable. I must have been out on that wing for some time. I didn't know what to do."

Not that Sagon had been faced with insoluble problems. He thought himself alone on board. The plane was burning. The fighters were still after it and spattering it with bullets. What Sagon was telling us was that he had felt no desire of any kind. He had felt nothing. He had time on his hands. He was floating in a sort of infinite leisure. And point by point I recognized the extraordinary sensation that now and then accompanies the imminence of death—a feeling of unexpected leisure, absolutely the contrary of the picture-book notion of breathless haste. Sagon had lain there on his wing, a creature flung out of the dimension of time.

"And then," he said, "I jumped. I made a bad job of it. I could feel myself twisting in the air and hesitated to pull the cord, thinking I might get tangled up in the 'chute. I waited until I had straightened out. I waited quite a long time."

What Sagon really remembered of his whole mishap, from beginning to end, was waiting. Waiting for the flames to rise higher. Then waiting on the wing for Heaven knows what. And finally, falling freely through the air, still waiting.

This was Sagon himself who was doing these things—actually a Sagon more rudimentary, more simple than the Sagon I know: a Sagon a little perplexed, bored and slightly impatient as he felt himself drop into an abyss.

VIII

WE HAD been living for two hours at the centre of an external pressure reduced to two thirds of normal. The crew were being gradually used up. We exchanged hardly a word. Once or twice, very cautiously, I tried to work my rudder. I was not obstinate about it. Each time the same sensation, the same feeling of a gentle exhaustion, had come over me.

Dutertre, at work with his camera, was careful to let me know in plenty of time when his photography required that I bank. I would do the best I could with such control of the wheel as was still left to me. I would tilt the plane and pull towards me; and in a dozen or twenty separate efforts I would set her where Dutertre wanted her.

"Altitude?"

"Thirty-three thousand seven."

"I see him exactly as he was, lying in the hospital bed." (PAGE 65)

I was still thinking of Sagon. Man is always himself. In myself I have never met another than myself. Sagon knew only Sagon. He who dies, dies as he was. In the death of an ordinary miner, it is an ordinary miner who dies. Where is it to be found—that haggard dementia that writers have invented to fascinate us with?

I saw once in Spain a man hauled up, after several days of excavation, out of the cellar of a house that had been destroyed by a bomb. He was blinking, for the daylight hurt his eyes; and men were holding him up, for he was tottering.

A crowd stood round him in silence and with what seemed to me a sudden timidity. This man, resuscitated almost from the beyond, still covered in the rubble in which he had been buried, half stupefied by suffocation and hunger, was like some dim monster. When some one grew bold enough to ask him questions, and to the questions he lent a kind of pallid attention, the timidity of the crowd changed to uneasiness.

Those round him tried to unlock his secret with bungling keys—for who is there can formulate the right question? They asked him what he had felt, what he had thought of, what he had done in that grave. They flung bridges at random across an abyss, like men seeking to reach the night of the mind of one blind and deaf and dumb, and bring him help. But when, finally, he was able to answer, what he said was, "Yes, I heard a long tearing sound." Or he said, "I was terribly worried. I was down there a long time. I thought it would never end." Or, "My back hurt. It hurt pretty badly." It was a decent fellow talking only about a decent fellow.

"I was worried about my watch," he said. "It was a wedding present. I couldn't get my hand into my pocket. I wondered if the cave-in had . . ."

It goes without saying that life had taught this man suffering and impatience, taught him the love of familiar things. He had made use of the man he was to take account of his universe, though it were the universe of a cave-in in the night. And the fundamental question, the question nobody thought of asking him but which governed all their blundering questions—"Who were you? Who surged up in you?"—this question he would have been unable to answer before time had allowed him little by little to build up the legend of himself. He would have been able to answer only—"Why, me . . . myself."

No single event can awaken within us a stranger totally unknown to us. To live is to be slowly born. It would be a bit too easy if we could go about borrowing ready-made souls.

It is true that a sudden illumination may now and then light up a destiny and impel a man in a new direction. But illumination is vision, suddenly granted the spirit, at the end of a long and gradual preparation. Bit by bit I learnt my grammar. I was taught my syntax. My sentiments were awakened. And now suddenly a poem strikes me in the heart.

Piloting now my plane, I feel no love; but if this evening something is revealed to me, it will be because I shall have carried my heavy stones towards the building of the invisible structure. I am preparing a celebration. I shall not have the right to speak of the sudden apparition in me of another than myself, since it is I who am struggling to awaken that other within me.

There is nothing that I may expect of the hazard of war except this slow apprenticeship. Like grammar, it will repay me later.

For us in the plane, life was losing its edge, blunted by a slow wearing away of ourselves. We were aging. The sortie was aging. What price high altitude? An hour of life spent at thirty-three thousand feet is equivalent to what? To a week? three weeks? a month of organic life, of the work of the heart, the lungs, the arteries? Not that it signifies. My semi-swoonings have added centuries to me: I float in the serenity of old age.

How far away now is the agitation in which I dressed! In what a distant past it is lost! And Arras is infinitely far in the future. The adventure of war? Where is there adventure in war? I have this day taken an even chance to disappear, and I have nothing to report unless it is that passage of tiny wasps seen for three seconds. The real adventure would have lasted but the tenth of a second; and those among us who go through it do not come back, never come back, to tell the story.

"Give her a kick to starboard, Captain."

Dutertre has forgotten that my rudder is frozen. I was thinking of a picture that used to fascinate me when I was a child. Against the background of an aurora borealis it showed a graveyard of fantastic ships, motionless in the Antarctic seas. In the ashen glow of an eternal night the ships raised their crystallized arms. The atmosphere was of death, but they still spread sails that bore the impress of the wind as a bed bears the impress of a shoulder, and the sails were stiff and cracking.

Here too everything was frozen. My controls were frozen. My machine-guns were frozen. And when I had asked the gunner about his, the answer had come back, "Nothing doing, sir."

Into the exhaust pipe of my mask I spat icicles fine as needles. From time to time I had to crush the stopper of frost that continued to form inside the flexible rubber, lest it suffocate me. When I squeezed the tube I felt it grate in my palm.

"Gunner! Oxygen all right?"

"Yes, sir."

"What's the pressure in the bottles?"

"Er . . . seventy. Falling, sir."

Time itself had frozen for us. We were three old men with white beards. Nothing was in motion. Nothing was urgent. Nothing was cruel.

The adventure of war. Major Alias had thought it necessary to say to me one day, "Take it easy, now!"

Take what easy, Major Alias? The fighters come down on you like lightning. Having spotted you from fifteen hundred feet above you, they take their time. They weave, they orient themselves, take careful aim. You know nothing of this. You are the mouse lying in the shadow of the bird of prey. The mouse fancies that it is alive. It goes on frisking in the wheat. But already it is the prisoner of the retina of the hawk, glued tighter to that retina than to any glue, for the hawk will never leave it now.

And thus you, continuing to pilot, to daydream, to scan the earth, have already been flung outside the dimension of time because of a tiny black dot on the retina of a man.

The nine planes of the German fighter group will drop like plummets in their own good time. They are in no hurry. At five hundred and fifty miles an hour they will fire their prodigious harpoon that never misses its prey. A bombing squadron possesses enough firing power to offer a chance for defense; but a reconnaissance crew, alone in the wide sky, has no chance against the seventy-two machine guns that first make themselves known to it by the luminous spray of their bullets. At the very instant when you first learn of its existence, the fighter, having spat forth its venom like a cobra, is already neutral and inaccessible, swaying to and fro overhead. Thus the cobra sways, sends forth its lightning, and resumes its rhythmical swaying.

Each machine-gun fires fourteen hundred bullets a

minute. And when the fighter group has vanished, still nothing has changed. The faces themselves have not changed. They begin to change now that the sky is empty and peace has returned. The fighter has become a mere impartial onlooker when, from the severed carotid in the neck of the reconnaissance pilot, the first jets of blood spurt forth. When from the hood of the starboard engine the hesitant leak of the first tongue of flame rises out of the furnace fire. And the cobra has returned to its folds when the venom strikes the heart and the first muscle of the face twitches. The fighter group does not kill. It sows death. Death sprouts after it has passed.

Take what easy, Major Alias? When we flew over those fighters I had no decision to make. I might as well not have known they were there. If they had been overhead, I should never have known it.

Take what easy? The sky is empty.

The earth is empty.

Look down on the earth from thirty-three thousand feet, and man ceases to exist. Man's traces are not to be read at this distance. Our telescopic lenses serve here as microscopes. It wants this microscope—not to photograph man, since he escapes even the telescopic lens—to perceive the signs of his presence. Highways, canals, convoys, barges. Man fructifies the microscope slide. I am a glacial scientist, and their war has become for me a laboratory experiment.

"Are the anti-aircraft firing, Dutertre?"

"I believe they are firing, Captain."

Dutertre cannot tell. The bursts are too distant and the smoke is blended in with the ground. They cannot hope to bring us down by such vague firing. At thirty-three thousand feet we are virtually invulnerable. They are firing in order to gauge our position, and probably also to guide the fighter groups towards us. A fighter group diluted in the sky like invisible dust.

The German on the ground knows us by the pearly white scarf which every plane flying at high altitude trails behind like a bridal veil. The disturbance created by our meteoric flight crystallizes the watery vapor in the atmosphere. We unwind behind us a cirrus of icicles. If the atmospheric conditions are favourable to the formation of clouds, our wake will thicken bit by bit and become an evening cloud over the countryside.

The fighters are guided towards us by their radio, by the bursts on the ground, and by the ostentatious luxury of our white scarf. Nevertheless we swim in an emptiness almost interplanetary. Everything round us and within us is total immobility.

We are now flying at three hundred and twenty-five miles an hour, you on the ground would say. But that is a race-course point of view. Here time is not, but only space. The earth itself, despite its twenty-five miles a second, moves but slowly round the sun. A whole year goes to the task. Perhaps we too are slowly approached in this exercise in gravitation. The density of aerial warfare? Grains of dust in a cathedral. We, grains of dust, are perhaps attracting to ourselves some dozens, it may be hundreds, of enemy grains of dust. And all those cinders rise as from a shaken rug slowly into the sky.

Take what easy, Major Alias? Looking straight down, all that I see is the bric-a-brac of another age exhibited under a pure crystal without tremor. I am leaning over the glass cases of a museum. But already the exhibit stands outlined against the light. Very far ahead lie Dunkerque and the sea. To left and right I see nothing. The sun has dropped too low, now, and I command the view of a vast glittering sheet.

"Dutertre! Can you see anything at all in this mess?"

"Straight down, yes."

"Gunner! Any sign of the fighters?"

"No sign, sir."

The fact is, I have absolutely no idea whether or not we are being pursued, and whether from the ground they can or cannot see us trailed by the collection of gossamer threads we sport.

Gossamer threads sets me day dreaming again. An image comes into my mind which for the moment seems to me enchanting. ". . . As inaccessible as a woman of exceeding beauty, we follow our destiny, drawing slowly behind us our train of frozen stars."

"A little kick to port, Captain."

There you have reality. But I go back to my shoddy

poetry: "We bank, and a whole sky of suitors banks in our wake."

Kick to port, indeed! Try it.

The woman of exceeding beauty has fumbled her bank.

Is it true that I was humming?

For Dutertre has spoken again. "Hum like that, Captain, and you'll pass out."

He has certainly killed my taste for humming.

"I've just about got all the photos I want, Captain. Another few minutes and we can make for Arras."

We can make for Arras. Why, of course. Since we're half way there, we might as well.

Phew! My throttles are frozen!

And I say to myself:

"This week, one crew out of three has got back. Therefore, there is great danger in this war. But if we are among those that get back, we shall have nothing to tell. I have had adventures—pioneering mail lines; being forced down among rebellious Arabs in the Sahara; flying the Andes. But war is not a true adventure. It is a mere ersatz. Where ties are established, where problems are set, where creation is stimulated—there you have adventure. But there is no adventure in heads-or-tails, in betting that the toss will come out life or death. War is not an adventure. It is a disease. It is like typhus."

Perhaps I shall feel later that my sole veritable adventure in this war was that of my room in Orconte.

IX

ORCONTE is a village on the outskirts of Saint-Dizier where my Group was stationed during the bitterly cold winter of '39. I was billeted in a clay-walled peasant house. The temperature would drop during the night low enough to freeze the water in my rustic crock, and the first thing I did in the morning was of course to light a fire. But to do that I had to get out of a bed in which I lay snug and warm and happy.

Nothing seemed to me more miraculous than that simple bed in that bare and freezing chamber. It was there that I revelled in the bliss of relaxation after the exhaustion of the day's work. I felt safe in that bed. No danger could reach me there. During the day I was exposed to the rigor of the upper altitudes and the risk of the peremptory machine guns. During the day my body was available for transformation into a lair of agony and undeserved laceration. During the day my body was not mine. Was no longer mine. Any of its members might at any moment be commandeered; its blood might at any moment be drawn off without my acquiescence. For it is another consequence of war that the soldier's body becomes a stock of accessories that are no longer his property. The bailiff arrives and demands a pair of eyes—you yield up the gift of sight. The bailiff arrives and demands a pair of legs—you yield up the gift of movement. The bailiff arrives torch in hand and demands the flesh off your face—and you, having yielded up the gift of smiling and manifesting your friendship for your kind, become a monster. Thus this body, which during any daylight hour might reveal itself my enemy and do me ill, might transform itself into a generator of whimperings, was still my obedient and comradely friend as it snuggled under the eiderdown in its demi-slumber, murmuring to my consciousness no more than its gratification and its purring bliss. Yet this body had to be withdrawn from beneath that eiderdown; it had to be washed in freezing water, shaved, dressed, made respectable before presenting itself to the bursts of steel. And getting out of bed was like a return to infancy, like being torn away from the maternal arms, the maternal breast, from everything that cherishes, caresses, shelters the existence of the infant.

So, having pondered and meditated and put off my decision as long as I could, I would grit my teeth and spring in a single leap to the fireplace, drench the logs with kerosene, and touch a match to them. Then, when the oil had flared up, and I had succeeded in crossing back to my bed, I would snuggle down again in its grateful warmth. With blankets and eiderdown drawn up to my left eye, I would watch the fireplace. At first the logs would seem not to catch, and only occasional flashes would flicker on the ceiling. But soon the fire would settle down in the hearth as if to organize a celebration. There would come a crackling, a roaring, a singing, and the fire would be as merry as a village wedding feast when the guests have begun to drink, to warm up, to nudge one another in the ribs.

Now and then it would seem to me that my good-tempered fire was standing guard over me like a particularly brisk and faithful shepherd dog going diligently about his work. A feeling of quiet jubilation would go through me as I watched it. And when the merry-making was at its height, when the shadows were dancing on the ceiling, when the warm golden music filled the air and the glowing logs had become a rosy architecture; when my room was quite redolent of the magic odor of smoke and resin, I would leap again from one friend to the other, from my bed to my fire; and standing there beside the more generous friend, I could never say whether I was in truth toasting my belly or warming my heart at that fireplace. Faced by two temptations, I like a coward had given way to the

stronger, the ruddier, the one which, with its fanfare
and flutter, had advertised its wares more cleverly.

Thus three times—first to light my fire, then to get
back into bed, then again to harvest my crop of flames
—three times with chattering teeth I had crossed the
bare and frozen tundra of my chamber and known what
it was to explore the polar regions. I had made my way
on foot across a desert to arrive at a blessed haven, and
my effort had been rewarded by that fire which in my
presence, for my sake, had danced its jubilant air.

Very likely my story seems to you pointless, and yet
this was a great adventure. My chamber had shown me
as in a glass something I should never have discovered
had I happened in by chance on this peasant house.
What, as tourist, I should have seen would have been a
bare and commonplace room, a vague bed, a water
pitcher, an ugly chimney-piece. I should have yawned
and turned away. Of its three provinces, its three civili-
zations—the one of sleep, the other of fire, the third of
desert—I should have known nothing, nor been able to
distinguish between them. How should I possibly have
guessed the adventure of the body—first as infant clinging to the tenderness and the shelter of the maternal
breast, then as soldier made for suffering, and finally as
man enriched by the delight of the civilization of fire—
fire, the magnetic pole of the tribe, that honors me and
will do honor to my comrades who, when they come
to see me if I get back, will take their part in this fes-
tivity, will draw up their chairs round mine, and while

we talk of our problems, our worries, our drudgery, will nevertheless say as they rub their hands and stuff their pipes, "There's no getting round it, a fire does make you feel fine."

But here in this plane there is no fire to persuade me to believe in friendship. There is no freezing chamber here to persuade me of the existence of adventure. I waken out of my reverie. There is nothing here but a void. Nothing but extreme old age. Nothing but a voice—Dutertre's, stubborn in its chimerical longing—saying to me:

"Give her a little kick to starboard, Captain."

X

I AM doing my job like a conscientious workman. Which does not alter the fact that I feel myself to be a pilot of defeat. I feel drenched in defeat. Defeat oozes out of every pore, and in my hands I hold a pledge of it.

For my throttle controls are frozen. The cold has turned them into two stumps of useless metal and has involved me in a serious predicament. For, whatever happens, I am forced to go on flying full throttle. Meanwhile, the pitch of my propellers, which serves in a sense as a brake on the revolution of my engines, is limited by an automatic check. If for any reason I am forced to dive, I shall be unable to reduce the speed of my engines, and unable also to increase my pitch. As I fall through space the torrential rush of air through my propellers will very likely increase the rotation of my engines to the point at which they blow up.

" . . . *that bare and freezing chamber.*"

(PAGE 82)

I could, if I had to, switch off my engines; but in that case I should never be able to start them again. I should then be stalled for good and all, which would mean the failure of the sortie and the crack-up of the machine. Not every terrain is favorable to the landing of a plane at one hundred and twenty miles an hour—and this, by manœuvering and gliding, is about the minimum speed at which I could hope to set the machine down. Therefore I must succeed in unblocking my throttles.

I was able to unblock the throttle of the port engine: the starboard throttle would not budge.

Now if I were forced down, I could reduce the speed of the port engine. But if I cut down the port engine, over which I have regained control, I should need to be able to offset the lateral traction exercised by the starboard engine—for the accelerated rotation of the starboard engine would obviously tend to pivot the plane to port. There is a way of offsetting this tendency. I could do it by the play of my rudder. But the bar that governs my rudder has long been frozen stiff. Therefore I should be able to offset nothing at all. The moment I cut down my port engine I must go into a spin.

Here was another of the war's absurdities. Nothing worked properly. Our world was made up of gear-wheels that would not mesh. And where the gear-wheels will not mesh, there is obviously no watchmaker.

After nine months of war we had still not succeeded in persuading the industries concerned that aerial cannon and controls ought to be manufactured with regard to the climate of the upper altitudes in which they were employed. What we were up against was not the irresponsible attitude of the manufacturers. Men are for the most part decent and conscientious. I am sure that almost always their seeming lack of initiative is a result and not a cause of their ineffectualness.

Ineffectualness weighed us down, all of us in the uniform of France, like a sort of doom. It hung over the infantry that stood with fixed bayonets in the face of German tanks. It lay upon the air crews that fought one against ten. It infected those very men whose job it should have been to see that our guns and controls did not freeze and jam.

We were living in the blind belly of an administration. An administration is a machine. The more perfect the machine, the more human initiative is eliminated from it. If, into a perfect machine, you introduce steel at one end, automobiles will come out of the other end. There will be no room for technical flaws, errors of measurement, human carelessness. And in a perfect administration, where man plays the part of a cog, such things as laziness, dishonesty, or injustice, cannot prevail.

But a machine is not built for creation. It is built for administration. It administers the transformation of steel into motor cars. It goes unvaryingly through motions pre-ordained once and for always. And an administration, like a machine, does not create. It carries on. It applies a given penalty to a given breach of the rules, a given method to a given aim. An administration is not conceived for the purpose of solving fresh problems. If, into your automobile-manufacturing machine, you inserted wood at one end, furniture would not come out at the other end. For this to happen, a man would have to intervene with authority to rip the whole thing up. But an administration is conceived as a safeguard against disturbances resulting from human initiative. The gearwheels of the watch stand guard against the intervention of man. The watchmaker has no place among them.

I was posted to Group 2-33 in November 1939. When I arrived, my fellow pilots gave me due warning.

"You'll be flying over Germany," they said, "without guns or controls."

And to console me, they added: "But don't take it too hard, for it really doesn't matter. The German fighters always down you before you know they are there."

Six months later, in May 1940, the guns and the controls were still freezing up.

In the spring of 1940, everybody was repeating an ancient French saw: "France is always saved at the eleventh hour by a miracle."

There was a reason for the miracle. It used to happen

occasionally that the beautiful administrative machine would break down and everybody would agree that it could not be repaired. For want of better, men would be substituted for the machine. And men would save France.

If a bomb had reduced the Air Ministry to ashes, a corporal—any corporal at all—would have been summoned, and the government would have said to him:

"You are ordered to see that the controls are thawed out. You have full authority. It's up to you. But if they are still freezing up two weeks from now you go to prison."

The controls would perhaps have been thawed out.

I could cite a hundred examples of this flaw. The Requisitions Committee for the Department of the North, for example, used to requisition heifers quick with young, and the slaughter-houses of France were transformed into graveyards of fœtuses. The requisitioning administration was a perfect machine. And because it was, not a single cog in the machine, not a single colonel on the board, had the slightest authority to act otherwise than as a cog. Each cog, as if the machine were a watch, was obedient to another cog. Revolt against the whole was useless. And this is why, once the machine began to go out of order, the cogs light heartedly took to slaughtering freshened heifers. It may have been the lesser evil. Had the machine broken down altogether, the cogs might have begun to slaughter colonels.

I sat at my wheel discouraged to the marrow of my bones by this universal dilapidation. But as it seemed to me useless to blow up one of my engines, I fought again with the starboard throttle. In my disgust I forgot myself, wrestled with it too strenuously, and had to give it up. The effort had cost me another twinge at the heart. It was obvious that man was not made to do physical culture exercises at thirty-three thousand feet in the air. That twinge of pain was a warning, a sort of localized consciousness queerly come to life in the night of my organs.

"Let the engines blow up if they want to," I said to myself, "I don't care a hang." I was trying to catch my breath. It seemed to me that if I took my mind off my breath I should never be able to catch it again. The image of a pair of old-fashioned bellows came into my mind. I am stirring up my fire, I thought. And I prayed that it would make up its mind to catch.

Was there something I had wrenched beyond repair? At thirty-three thousand feet a slightly strenuous physical effort can strain the heart muscles. A heart is a frail thing. It has to go on working a long time. It is silly to endanger it for such coarse work. As if one burnt up diamonds in order to bake a potato.

XI

AS IF one burnt up all the villages of France without by their destruction halting the German advance for a single day. And yet this stock of villages, this heritage, these ancient churches, these old houses with all the cargo of memories they carry, with their shining floors of polished walnut, the white linen in their cupboards, the laces at their windows that have served unfrayed so many generations—here they are burning from Alsace to the sea.

Burning is a great word when you look down from thirty-three thousand feet; for over the villages and the forests there is nothing to be seen but a pall of motionless smoke, a sort of ghastly whitish jelly. Below it the fires are at work like a secret digestion. At thirty-three thousand feet time slows down, for there is no movement here. There are no crackling flames, no crashing beams, no spirals of black smoke. There is only that

96

grayish milk curdled in the amber air. Will that forest recover? Will that village recover? Seen from this height. France is being undermined by the secret gnawing of bacteria.

About this, too, there is much to be said. "We shall not hesitate to sacrifice our villages." I have heard these words spoken. And it was necessary to speak them. When a war is on, a village ceases to be a cluster of traditions. The enemy who hold it have turned it into a nest of rats. Things no longer mean the same. Here are trees three hundred years old that shade the home of your family. But they obstruct the field of fire of a twenty-two-year-old lieutenant. Wherefore he sends up a squad of fifteen men to annihilate the work of time. In ten minutes he destroys three hundred years of patience and sunlight, three hundred years of the religion of the home and of betrothals in the shadows round the grounds. You say to him, "My trees!" but he does not hear you. He is right. He is fighting a war.

But how many villages have we seen burnt down only that war may be made to look like war? Burnt down exactly as trees are cut down, crews flung into the holocaust, infantry sent against tanks, merely to make war look like war. Small wonder that an unutterable disquiet hangs over the land. For nothing does any good.

One fact the enemy grasped and exploited—that men fill small space in the earth's immensity. A continuous wall of men along our front would require a hundred million soldiers. Necessarily, there were always gaps between the French units. In theory, these gaps are cancelled by the mobility of the units. Not, however, in the theory of the armored division, for which an almost unmotorized army is as good as unmanœuvrable. The gaps are real gaps. Whence this simple tactical rule: "An armored division should move against the enemy like water. It should bear lightly against the enemy's wall of defence and advance only at the point where it meets with no resistance." The tanks operate by this rule, bear against the wall, and never fail to break through. They move as they please for want of French tanks to set against them; and though the damage they do is superficial,—capture of unit Staffs, cutting of telephone cables, burning of villages,— the consequences of their raids are irreparable. In every region through which they make their lightning sweep, a French army, even though it seem to be virtually intact, has ceased to be an army. It has been transformed into clotted segments. It has, so to say, coagulated. The armored divisions play the part of a chemical agent precipitating a colloidal solution. Where once an organism existed they leave a mere sum of organs whose unity has been destroyed. Between the clots—however combative the clots may have remained—the enemy moves at will. An army, if it is to be effective, must be something other than a numerical sum of soldiers.

We stand to the enemy in the relation of one man to three. One plane to ten or twenty. After Dunkerque, one tank to one hundred. We have no time to meditate

upon the past; no time to say to ourselves even this—
that forty million farmers must lose an armament race
run against eighty million industrial workers. We are
engaged in the present. And the present is what it is. No
sacrifice, at any moment, on any front, can serve to slow
up the German advance.

Whence it comes that throughout the civil and military hierarchies, from the plumber to the minister of
State, from the second-class private to the general, there
reigns a sort of uneasiness which no one can or dares
put into words. There is no dignity in sacrifice if it is
mere parody or suicide. It is beautiful to sacrifice oneself. These die in order that the rest be saved. The flames
are grimly fought when the conflagration has to be put
out. Men fight to the death in the cut-off camp so that
their rescuers may have time to come to their aid. Yes,
but we are surrounded by the conflagration. We have
no camp on which to fall back. We know no rescuers on
whom we can pin our hope. And as for those for whom
we fight, for whom we say we are fighting, what are
we doing except, apparently, ensuring their murder?
For the aeroplane, dropping its bombs on towns behind
the lines, has made this such a war as was never
dreamt of.

I was later to hear foreigners reproach France with
the few bridges that were not blown up, the handful of
villages we did not burn, the men who failed to die.

But here on the scene, it is the contrary, it is exactly the contrary, that strikes me so powerfully. It is our desperate struggle against self-evident fact. We know that nothing can do any good, yet we blow up bridges nevertheless, in order to play the game. We burn down real villages, in order to play the game. It is in order to play the game that our men die.

Of course some are overlooked! Bridges are overlooked, villages are overlooked, men are allowed to continue alive. But the tragedy of this rout is that all its acts are without meaning. The soldier who blows up a bridge can only do it reluctantly. He slows down no enemy—he merely creates a ruined bridge. He destroys his country in order to turn it into a splendid caricature of war. But it was a real bridge, not a caricature, that was blown up.

If a man is to strive with all his heart, the significance of his striving must be unmistakable. The significance of the ashes of the village must be as telling as the significance of the village itself. But the ashes of our villages are meaningless. Our dead must be as meaningful as death itself. But our dead die in a charade. The enemy's hundred and sixty divisions are not impressed by our burnings and our dead.

The question used to be asked, Are our men dying well or badly? Meaningless question! The Staff know that a given town can hold out for three hours. Yet our men are ordered to hold it forever. Having no means of offense, they as good as beg the enemy to destroy the town in order that the rules of war be respected.

They are like a friendly opponent at chess who says, "But you have forgotten to take your pawn." Our men spend their time challenging the enemy.

"We are the defenders of the village," they say in effect. "You are the attackers. Ready? Play!"

And under the burst of an enemy squadron the village is wiped out.

"Well played, Nazi!"

Certainly inert men exist, but inertia is frustrated despair. Certainly fugitives exist, and I remember that twice or three times Major Alias had threatened to shoot occasional gloomy wretches picked up on the highways and evasive in the answers they gave to his questions. One's impulse is so strong to make somebody responsible for disaster, and to believe that by putting him out of the way all can be saved. The fugitives are responsible for the rout, since there would be no rout if there were no fugitives. Therefore, flourish a gun and all is well.

As well bury the sick in order to eliminate sickness. Major Alias always ended by slipping his gun back into its holster. He could see very well that there was something awfully pompous about that gun, like a comic-opera saber. Alias knew perfectly well that those mournful fellows were an effect, not a cause of the disaster. He knew absolutely that they were the same men, exactly the same men, as those who, somewhere else in France, at that very moment, were accepting the fact that they must die. In two short weeks one hundred and fifty thousand of them accepted the fact that they must die. But some men are stubborn and insist upon a reason why they should die.

It is hard to find a reason.

Here is a runner engaged in the race of life against other runners of his own class. The starter fires, the runner springs forward—and he discovers that he has a ball and chain attached to his leg. He quits.

"This race doesn't count," he says.

"It does though, it does!" you protest.

What are you going to tell a man to make him put his heart into a race that is not a race? Alias knew what those fugitives were thinking. "This race doesn't count," was what they were thinking.

Alias put his gun back into the holster and tried to find a better argument.

There is but one better argument, but one logical argument, and I challenge anybody to find another. It is this: "Your death will have no effect at all. Defeat is inescapable. But it is proper that a defeat manifest itself by dead. There must be mourning. Your part is to play the dead."

"Very good, sir."

Alias did not despise the fugitives. He knew well enough that his argument always worked. He himself accepted the expectancy of death. All his crews accepted the expectancy of death. His argument, slightly disguised, never failed to work with us: "It's damned awkward. But the General Staff want it done. They very much want it done. . . . And that's that."

"Very good, sir."

Alias knew that we had accepted.

My very simple notion is that those who died served as bondsmen for the rest.

XII

I HAVE aged so much that all that I was is left behind me. I stare out through the great glittering plate of my windscreen. Below me are men. Infusoria wriggling under a microscope. Who can work up interest in a family of infusoria?

Were it not for this twinge of pain that seems to me a living thing, I could sink into drowsy rumination, like an aged tyrant. It is only ten minutes since I spoke of our crews as supernumeraries. Pure rhetoric and sickeningly false. When I saw the German fighters below, did my fancy speak of tender sighs? It spoke of poisonous wasps. That was reality. They were tiny, and they were obscene. It is hard to believe that I invented that disgusting literary image of a dress with a train. I couldn't have! For one thing, I have never seen the wake of my ship. Here in this cockpit, in which I fit like a pipe in its case, I can see nothing behind me. I see behind me through the eyes of my gunner. And then only if the inter-com is working. My gunner never called down to me, "Adoring suitors aft in the wake of our train!"

All this is mere juggling with words. Of course I should like to believe, I should like to fight, I should like to win. But try as a man will to pretend to believe, pretend to fight, pretend to win by setting fire to his own villages, it is hard to feel elation over pretense.

It is hard to exist. Man is a knot into which relationships are tied, and my ties serve me hardly at all.

What is this in me that has broken down? What is the secret of substitutions? Whence comes it that a gesture, a word, can give rise to endless ripples in a human destiny? Whence comes it that in other circumstances I should be overwhelmed by what seems to me now remote and abstract? Whence comes it that if I were Pasteur, the play of true infusoria would seem to me pathetic to the point where a slide under a microscope would represent something infinitely more vast than a virgin forest, and the watching of that slide would seem to me the most thrilling kind of adventure? Whence comes it that that black dot below, which is a house of men. . . .

But again a childhood memory returns to me.

When I was a small boy. . . . I speak of my early childhood, that is to say, of a vast region out of which all men

" . . . *under the burst of an enemy squadron the village is wiped out.*" (PAGE 101)

emerge. Whence come I? I come from my childhood.
I come from childhood as from a homeland. . . . When
I was a small boy, then, I had a queer experience.

I must have been five or six years old. It was eight in
the evening. At eight o'clock children ought to be
in bed. Particularly in winter, when night has already
fallen. For some reason I had been forgotten.

On the ground floor of our house in the country—
which was big—there was a hall that seemed to me immense. It led into the warm room at the back in which
we children were fed our supper. I had always been
afraid of that hall, perhaps because of the feeble light
of the lamp that hung in the middle of it and scarcely
drew it forth from the darkness. A signal rather than a
light. The hall was paneled high up, and the paneling
creaked, which was another reason for my fear. And it
was cold. Coming into it out of the warm and lamplit
rooms that lined it was like coming into a cavern.

But that evening, seeing that I had been forgotten, I
gave way to the demon of evil in me, reached up on tip-
toe for the handle of our supper-room door, pushed the
door softly in, and embarked upon my illicit exploration
of the world.

The creaking of the paneling was the first warning I
received of heavenly anger. I could see in the shadow the
great reproving panels. Not daring to explore farther, I
climbed up on a console table, and there, resting against
the wall and letting my legs hang, I sat with beating

heart like every shipwrecked sailor before me on his reef in mid-sea.

At that moment the drawing-room door opened. Two uncles who absolutely terrified me shut the door behind them upon the lights and the hubbub of voices, and began to pace the hall.

I trembled lest I be discovered. Uncle Hubert was in my eyes the very image of severity. A delegate of divine justice. This man, who never in his life had tweaked a child's ear or pinched its cheek affectionately, always threatened me when I had been naughty with a terrifying frown and these words: "The next time that I go to America I shall bring back a whipping machine. American machines are the most modern in the world. That is why American children are the best behaved in the world. And a very good thing for their parents, too."

I did not like America.

Here they were, then, strolling back and forth through the interminable hall while I almost fainted. holding my breath and following them with my eyes and ears. "In times like these," they said; and they moved off with their secret meant only for grown people. "In times like these," I memorized the phrase. Then, as if a tide had rolled up to me another of its indecipherable treasures—"It's pure madness, positive madness," one uncle said to the other. And I fished up that phrase as if it were a priceless thing, and to myself I said slowly, testing its power upon the consciousness of a five-year-old, "It's pure madness, positive madness."

The tide carried my uncles away, the tide rolled them up again. With a kind of sidereal regularity, like a gravitational phenomenon, this going and coming repeated itself and suggested to me fitfully lighted glimpses of the life of man. I was marooned on my console for eternity, the clandestine listener to a solemn consultation in the course of which my uncles, who knew all there was to know, were collaborating in the creation of the world. The house might stand a thousand years: for all that thousand years my two uncles, pacing the hall with the patience of a pendulum, would continue to fill the air with the apprehension of eternity.

That black dot at which I stare is surely a human habitation thirty-three thousand feet below me. And I receive nothing from it. Yet it is possibly a great country house, and there may be two uncles in it pacing to and fro and slowly constructing in the consciousness of a child something as fabulous as the immensity of the seas.

My field of vision embraces a territory as large as a province, yet round me space has shrunk to the point of suffocation. In all this space I have less space at my disposal than was available to me in the replica of that black dot. I have lost the sense of distance, am blind to distance. But I feel now a kind of thirst for it. And it seems to me that I have stumbled here upon a common denominator of all the aspirations of mankind.

When chance awakens love, everything takes its place in a man in obedience to that love, and love brings him the sense of distance. When, in the Sahara, the Arabs would surge up in the night round our campfires and warn us of a coming danger, the desert would spring to life for us and take on meaning. Those messengers had lent it distance. Music does something like this. The humble odor of an old cupboard does it when it awakens and brings memories to life. Pathos is the sense of distance.

But I know that nothing which truly concerns man is calculable, weighable, measurable. True distance is not the concern of the eye; it is granted only to the spirit. Its value is the value of language, for it is language which binds things together.

And now it seems to me that I begin to see what a civilization is. A civilization is a heritage of beliefs, customs, and knowledge slowly accumulated in the course of centuries, elements difficult at times to justify by logic, but justifying themselves as paths when they lead somewhere, since they open up for man his inner distance.

There is a cheap literature that speaks to us of the need of escape. It is true that when we travel we are in search of distance. But distance is not to be found. It melts away. And escape has never led anywhere. The moment a man finds that he must play the races, go to the Arctic, or make war in order to feel himself alive, that man has begun to spin the strands that bind him to other men and to the world. But what wretched strands! A civilization that is really strong fills man to the brim, though he never stir. What are we worth when motionless, is the question.

There is a density of being in a Dominican at prayer. He is never so much alive as when prostrate and motionless before his God. In Pasteur, holding his breath over the microscope, there is a density of being. Pasteur is never more alive than in that moment of scrutiny. At that moment he is moving forward. He is hurrying. He is advancing in seven-league boots, exploring distance despite his immobility. Cézanne, mute and motionless before his sketch, is an inestimable presence. He is never more alive than when silent, when feeling and pondering. At that moment his canvas becomes for him something wider than the seas.

Distance granted man by the childhood home, by the chamber at Orconte, by the field of vision of Pasteur's microscope; distance opened up by a poem. What are these but the fragile and magical gifts that only a civilization is able to distribute? For distance is the property of the spirit, not of the eye; and there is no distance without language.

But how am I to quicken the sense of my language when all is confusion? When the trees round the house are at one and the same time a ship transporting the generations of a family and a mere screen in the way of an artilleryman? When the press of the German bombers bearing down upon the villages has squeezed out a whole people and sent it flowing down the highways like a black syrup? When France displays the sordid disorder of a scattered ant-hill? When we must fight, not against a flesh-and-blood opponent, but against rudders that freeze, throttles that jam, bolts that stick?

"You may drop down now, Captain."

I may drop down. I shall drop down. I shall drop down upon Arras. I shall carry out the second half of our mission—the low-altitude sortie. Behind me I have a thousand years of civilization to help me. But they have not helped me yet. I dare say this is not the moment for rewards.

At five hundred miles an hour I lose altitude. Banking, I have left behind me a polar sun exaggeratedly red. Ahead and three or four miles below me, I see the broad surface of a rectilinear mass of cloud that looks like an ice-floe. A whole province of France lies buried in its shadow. Arras lies shadowed by it. Beneath my ice-floe, I imagine, the world has a blackish tinge. The war must be stewing there as in the belly of a giant soup-kettle. Jammed roads, flaming houses, tools lying where they were flung down, villages in ruins, muddle, endless muddle.

To drop down here is like tumbling into a ruin. We shall have to splash about in their mud. We shall have to live with those below in their barbarous dilapidation.

Below us lies a world in decomposition. We are like travelers who, after long years amid coral and palm, are on our way home penniless. We face the prospect of a return to our native sordidness—the greasy food of avaricious relatives, the cantankerousness of family squabbles, the bad conscience born of money cares, the disappointed hopes, the degrading flight before the rent-collector, the arrogance of the landlord; squalor, and the stinking death in hospital. Up here at any rate death is clean. A death of flame and ice. Of sun and sky and flame and ice. But below! That digestion stewing in slime . . .

XIII

DUTERTRE'S voice came down the inter-com.
"Due south, Captain."

Quite right. Safer to lose altitude over our own
zone than the enemy's.

Looking down on those swarming highways I understood more clearly than ever what peace meant. In time
of peace the world is self-contained. The villagers come
home at dusk from their fields. The grain is stored up in
the barns. The folded linen is piled up in the cupboards.
In time of peace each thing is in its place, easily found.
Each friend is where he belongs, easily reached. All
men know where they will sleep when night comes.
Ah, but peace dies when the framework is ripped apart.
When there is no longer a place that is yours in the
world. When you know no longer where your friend
is to be found. Peace is present when man can see the
face that is composed of things that have meaning and

are in their place. Peace is present when things form part of a whole greater than their sum, as the divers minerals in the ground collect to become the tree.

But this is war.

I can see from my plane the long swarming highways, that interminable syrup flowing endless to the horizon. The inhabitants of the war zone are being evacuated. This, at any rate, is the official version. But it is no longer true. They are evacuating themselves. There is a crazy contagion in this exodus. Where are these vagabonds going? They are going south—as if in the south there was room for them, food for them, tender hands waiting to welcome them. But southward there are only villages filled to bursting, men and women sleeping in sheds, stocks of food running out. Southward the most generous hearts are beginning little by little to harden at the sight of this mad invasion which little by little, like a sluggish river of mud, is beginning to suffocate them. Can a single province lodge and nourish all France?

Where are they going? They have no notion. They are tramping towards phantom havens—for scarcely does this caravan come up to an oasis when it ceases to be an oasis. One by one each oasis bursts its bonds and pours into the caravan. And when, by chance, the caravan comes upon a real village, a village that seems still to be alive, it swallows up its substance in a single night, gnaws it clean as the worm polishes the bone.

Faster than the exodus, the enemy moves. Here and there armored cars roll past the stream. It thickens, swirls, flows for a moment backwards. Whole German divisions flounder in this stew; and Germans who at another point were killing their kind are here quenching the thirst of the refugees.

In the course of the retreat our Group had been quartered in a dozen villages. A dozen times our Group had been entangled in the dragging herd that shuffled slowly through those villages.

"Where are you bound?"

"Nobody knows."

They never knew. Nobody knew anything. They were ¬vacuating. There was no way to house them. Every road was blocked. And still they were evacuating. Somewhere in the north of France a boot had scattered an ant-hill, and the ants were on the march. Laboriously. Without panic. Without hope. Without despair. On the march as if in duty bound.

"Who ordered you to evacuate?"

It was always the mayor, or the schoolteacher, or the mayor's clerk. One morning at three the order had run through the village:

"Everybody out!"

They had been expecting this. For two weeks they had seen the passage through their village of refugees who no longer believed in the eternity of their homes. Man had been a settler on the planet. He had ceased to be a nomad. He had built himself villages that had lasted through the ages. He had waxed and polished floors and chairs that had gone on serving his great-grandchildren. The family house had received him at his birth, transported him to his death; and then, like a good bark crossing the water from bank to bank, it had carried his sons over the same stream. All that was ended now. The villagers were on the move. And no one so much as knew why.

The highways too were part of our experience. We were pilots, and there were days when in a single morning our sortie took us over Alsace, Belgium, Holland, and the sea itself. But our problems were most often of the north of France, and our horizon was very often limited to the dimensions of a traffic tangle at a crossroads. Thus, only three days earlier, I had seen the village in which we were billeted go to pieces. I do not expect ever to be free of that clinging, viscous memory.

It was six in the morning, and Dutertre and I, coming out of our billet, found ourselves in the midst of chaos. All the stables, all the sheds, all the barns and garages had vomited into the narrow streets a most extraordinary collection of contrivances. There were new motorcars, and there were ancient farm carts that for half a century had stood untouched under layers of dust. There were hay wains and lorries, carry alls and tumbrils. Had we seen a mail-coach in this maze it would not have astonished us. Every box on wheels had been dug up and was now laden with the treasures of the home. From door to vehicle, wrapped in bedsheets sagging with hernias, the treasures were being piled in.

Together, these treasures had made up that greater treasure—a home. By itself, each was valueless; yet they were the objects of a private religion, a family's worship. Each filling its place, they had been made indispensable by habit and beautiful by memory, had been lent price by the sort of fatherland which, together, they constituted. But those who owned them thought each precious in itself and for itself. These treasures had been wrenched from their fireside, their table, their wall; and now that they were heaped up in disorder, they showed themselves to be the worn and torn stock of a junk-shop that they were. Fling sacred relics into a heap, and they can turn your stomach.

"What's going on here? Are you mad?"

The café owner's wife shrugged her shoulders.

"We're evacuating."

"But why, in God's name!"

"Nobody knows. Mayor's orders."

She was too busy to talk, and vanished up her staircase. Dutertre and I stood in the doorway and looked on. Every motor car, every lorry, every cart and charabanc was piled high with children, mattresses, kitchen utensils.

Of all these objects the most pitiful were the old motorcars. A horse standing upright in the shafts of a farm-cart gives off a sensation of solidity. A horse does not call for spare parts. A farm-cart can be put into shape with three nails. But all these vestiges of the mechanical age! This assemblage of pistons, valves, magnetoes, and gear-wheels! How long would it run before it broke down?

"Please, captain. Could you give me a hand?"

"Of course. What is it?"

"I want to get my car out of the garage."

I looked at the woman in amazement.

"Are you sure you know how to drive?"

"Oh, it will be all right. The road is so jammed, it won't be hard."

There was herself, and her sister-in-law, and their children—seven children in all.

That road easy to drive? A road over which you made two or ten miles a day, stopping dead every two hundred yards? Braking, stopping, shifting gears, changing from low into second and back again every fifty yards in the confusion of an inextricable jam. Easy driving? The woman would break down before she had gone half a mile! And gas! And oil! And water, which she was sure to forget!

"Better watch your water. Your radiator is leaking like a sieve."

"Well, it's not a new car."

"You'll be on the road a week, you know. How are you going to make it?"

"I don't know."

She won't have gone three miles before running into half a dozen cars, stripping her gears, and blowing out her tires. Then she and her sister-in-law and the seven children will start to cry. And she and her sister-in-law and the seven children, faced by problems out of their ken, will give up. They will abandon the car, sit down by the side of the road, and wait for the coming of a shepherd.

But it is astonishing how few shepherds there are. Dutertre and I are staring at sheep who have taken things into their own hands. And these sheep are off in an immense clatter of mechanical equipment. Three thousand pistons. Six thousand valves. The grate, the grind, the clank of this machinery. Water boiling up in a radiator already. And slowly, laboriously, this caravan of doom stirs into movement. This caravan without spare parts, without tires, without gasoline, without a mechanic. They are mad!

"Why don't you stay home?"

"God knows, we'd rather stay."

"Then why do you leave?"

"They said we had to."

"Who said so?"

"The mayor."

Always the mayor.

"Of course we'd all rather stay home."

It is a fact that these people are not panicky; they are people doing a blind chore. Dutertre and I tried to shake some of them out of it.

"Look here, why don't you unload and put that stuff

back into your house. At least you'll have your pump-water to drink."

"Of course that would be the best thing."

"But you are free to do it. Why don't you?"

Dutertre and I are winning. A cluster of villagers has collected round us. They listen to us. They nod their heads approvingly.

"He's right, he is, the captain."

Others come to our support. A roadmender, converted, is hotter about it than I am.

"Always said so. Get out on that road and there's nothing but asphalt to eat."

They argue. They agree. They will stay. Some go off to preach to others. And they come back discouraged.

"Won't do. Have to go."

"Why?"

"Baker's already left. Who will bake our bread?"

The village has already broken down. At one point or another it has burst; and through that hole its contents are running out. Hopeless.

Dutertre said what he thought about it:

"The tragedy is that men have been taught that war is an abnormal condition. In the past they would have stayed home. War and life were the same thing."

The café owner came down, dragging a sack.

"You can let us have a cup of coffee, I suppose. We are flying in half an hour."

"Ah, my poor lads!"

"Somewhere in the north of France a boot had scattered an ant-hill and the ants were on the march." (PAGE 118)

She wiped her eyes. It was not us she was weeping for. Nor herself. Already she was crying with exhaustion. Already she felt herself suffocating in that caravan which was to go further to pieces with every mile of its journey.

Farther on, in the open country, the enemy fighters would be flying low and spitting forth their bursts of machine-gun fire upon this lamentable flock. But it was astonishing how on the whole the enemy refrained from total annihilation. Here and there stood a car in flames, but very few. And there were few dead. Death was a sort of luxury, something like a bit of advice. It was the nip in the hock by which the shepherd dog hurried the flock along. Though one wondered why the enemy action was so little insistent, so altogether sporadic and local. The enemy was at no pains whatever to blow the caravan to bits. True, the caravan had no need of the enemy to go to pieces. The machines took care of that. They went spontaneously out of order. The machine is conceived for a deliberate and peaceful society, a society master of its time. When man is not present to repair the machine, regulate it, polish it, it ages at a dizzying pace. Tonight all these machines will look a thousand years old. I seemed to be looking on at the death-throes of the machine.

Here is a peasant whipping up his horse. Perched on his seat with the majesty of a king, he lords it over the whole caravan.

"You look very satisfied up there."

"Ah, it's the end of the world."

Suddenly I felt queasy. All these workers, these simple people, each with his place in the world, were to be transformed into parasites, vermin. They were going to spread over the countryside and devour it. The thought made me sick.

"Who is going to feed you?"

"Nobody knows."

How is one to feed millions of migrants shuffling over miles of road at the rate of two to ten miles a day? If food existed, it could not be brought up to them.

All this muddle of men and old iron lost on the asphalt of the highways made me think suddenly of my march through the Libyan desert. Prévot and I had crashed in a landscape glassy with black rocks and covered with a carpet of sun-grilled iron. This was not far different.

I stared at the refugees in despair. How long would a swarm of locusts last in a field of asphalt?

"Do you expect to drink rain-water?"

"Nobody knows."

They knew nothing. For ten days they had seen an unbroken stream of refugees from the north flow through their village. For ten days they had watched this unending exodus. And their turn had come. They would take their place in the procession. But without confidence:

"If it was up to me, I'd rather die at home."

"We'd all rather die at home."

That was true. Their village might have collapsed over their heads, and still none would have chosen to leave.

Had France possessed reserves of food, that food could never have been brought up the highways down which this stream was flowing. If you have to, you can force your way downstream through brokendown cars, jammed cars, inextricable snarls of traffic at successive crossroads. But how can you move against such a stream?

"There being no reserves of food," said Dutertre grimly, "all is well."

A rumor is spreading that the Government has forbidden all evacuations. Even if it were true, how were the orders to be transmitted? There are no open roads, and the telephone cables are jammed, or cut; or the messages are received with a distrust born of experience. And it is no longer a matter of giving orders. What is wanted is the invention of a new code. For a thousand years man has been taught that women and children are to be shielded from war. War is a matter for men only. The village mayors are full of this law of society; their clerks know it; the schoolteachers know it. Assume that suddenly they receive orders to stop the evacuations, which is to say, force women and children to remain in the zone of bombardment. It will take them a month to adjust their conscience to this sign of a new age. You cannot overthrow a system of morality at one blow. And while you examine your conscience, the enemy continues his advance. Wherefore the mayors, their clerks, the schoolteachers send forth this stream of people on the highways. What is to be done? Where does truth reside? Forward troop the sheep without shepherd.

"Is there a doctor in this village?"

"You don't live here, I take it?"

"No. We live up north."

"What do you want of a doctor?"

"My wife is going to have a baby."

Lying among her kitchen utensils, in this desert of old iron.

"Couldn't you have thought of a doctor earlier?"

"We've been four days on the road."

The road is an irresistible stream. Where can you stop? Every village you move through is deserted the moment you arrive, pours into the caravan like the flow of a burst pipe into a giant sewer.

"No. No doctor here. The Group doctor is ten miles up the line."

"Well. Thank you."

The man mopped his forehead. Everything was going to pieces. His wife would bring her child into the world in a bed of kitchen utensils. There was nothing cruel about this. It was above all, most of all, monstrously beyond the bounds of things human. Nobody complained. Complaint was meaningless. His wife would die, and he would not complain. His wife was to die in childbed. Complain of what? There was no help for it. It was a nightmare.

"If we could only stop somewhere!"

Find a real village, a real inn, a real hospital. But, for God knows what reason, the hospitals too are being evacuated. It is part of the game. There isn't time to re-cast the rules of the game. Find a real death. But there is no real death any longer. There are bodies that break down the way the cars do.

Everywhere in this mob I sense a wearied haste, a haste that has renounced haste. At the rate of two to ten miles a day these people are fleeing before tanks moving at fifty miles a day and aeroplanes flying at four hundred miles an hour. Thus treacle flows when the bottle has been overturned. This man's wife would lie in; but he had all the time in the world before him. It was urgent. Was it really urgent? It was suspended in unstable equilibrium between urgency and eternity.

The world of these people had slowed down, like the reflexes of a dying man. This was an enormous flock that stood, exhausted and shuffling, at the gates of a slaughter-house. Were there ten or only five million of them on the asphalt? Here was a people accepting the notion of its reabsorption into eternity.

"How," I said to myself, "are these people to survive? Man does not eat branches." But they themselves were not in the least horrified by their fate. Wrenched from their homes, their work, their responsibilities, they had lost all significance. Their very identity seemed to have been rubbed off. They were very little themselves. They were very little alive. Later, they would re-invent their sufferings. Meanwhile they were suffering most of all from the aching strain of heavy loads, from the loosened knots in bedsheets that dripped with their dreary entrails, from the strain of pushing motorcars forward in the attempt to make the engines turn over.

Not a word about defeat. Naturally. No man feels the need of discussing a thing which constitutes his very substance. They *were* the defeat. I had suddenly the vision of a France losing its entrails. Quick! Sew up our France! There is not a moment to lose! France is doomed.

It began again. Like fish on dry land, these people were suffocating:

"Anybody got any milk here?"

A question to make you die laughing.

"My kid hasn't drunk anything since yesterday."

The kid was a six-months-old baby. He made a lot of noise. But his noise wouldn't last. Fish out of water are soon quiet. There is no milk here. There is only scrap-iron here. There is only an enormous quantity of useless scrap-iron, falling apart mile after mile, dropping bolts, nuts, screws, sheets, while it bears this prodigiously needless exodus, this people, away towards oblivion.

A rumor spreads that some miles to the south the road is being machine-gunned by the enemy. There is talk of bombs. There is even the muffled sound of distant explosions. The rumor is no mere rumor.

But these people are not frightened. They seem even to perk up a little at the news. That concrete risk seems to them healthier than this drowning in old iron.

Ah, the blueprint that historians will draft of all this! The angles they will plot to lend shape to this mess! They will take the word of a cabinet minister, the decision of a general, the discussion of a committee, and out of that parade of ghosts they will build historic conversations in which they will discern farsighted views and weighty responsibilities. They will invent agreements, resistances, attitudinous pleas, cowardices. But I know what an evacuated ministry can be. I've seen one. It taught me that once a government evacuates, it is no longer a government. It is like a human body. If you begin to take it apart, sending the stomach here, the liver there, the guts somewhere else, that collection no longer constitutes an organism. I spent twenty minutes at the Air Ministry. And I can tell you that in time of evacuation a minister is a being who controls the movements of his messenger. Miraculous control. He has only to press a button. An electric cord still joins the flunkey to the minister. The minister presses the button and the flunkey appears.

"My car," says the minister.

And there his authority stops. He gives his flunkey a

little exercise. But the flunkey is not sure if, on earth, there exists a car that is the minister's. No electric cord runs between the flunkey and anything at all. The chauffeur is lost somewhere, out in the world. What could the men who governed us know of the war? Situated as we were, impossible as liaison now was, it would take our people a week to arrange for the bombardment of an enemy division spotted by my Group. What sound could reach the ears of our governors from this land that was losing its entrails? News moved at the rate of ten miles a day. The telephone service was out. There was no way of transmitting a picture of this being, this France, in a state of decomposition. The Government swam in a void, a polar void. From time to time it was reached by desperately urgent appeals; but they were abstract, reduced to three scrawled lines. How could those who governed us know whether ten million Frenchmen had or had not already died of hunger? And this cry for help from ten million men could have been contained in a single sentence. It wants but a single sentence to say:

"Meet you tomorrow at four."

Or:

"They say ten million men are dead."

Or:

"Blois is in flames."

Or:

"They've found your chauffeur."

All this on the same level of importance. Just like that.

Ten million men. The motorcar. The Army of the East. Western civilization. The chauffeur has been found. England. Bread. What time is it?

I give you seven letters. They are the seven letters of the Bible. Reproduce the Bible with them for me.

Historians will forget reality. They will invent thinking men, joined by mysterious fibers to an intelligible universe, possessed of sound farsighted views and pondering grave decisions according to the purest laws of Cartesian logic. There will be powers of good and powers of evil. Heroes and traitors. But treason implies responsibility for something, control over something, influence upon something, knowledge of something. Treason in our time is a proof of genius. Why, I want to know, are not traitors decorated?

XIV

ALREADY as I move in the direction of Arras, peace is everywhere beginning to take shape. Not that well-defined peace which, like a new period in history, follows upon a war decorously terminated by a treaty. This is a nameless peace that stands for the end of everything. For an end of things that go on endlessly ending. It is an impulse that little by little finds itself bogged down. There is no feeling that either a good or a bad conclusion is on the way. Quite the contrary. Little by little the notion that this putrefaction is provisional gives way to the feeling that it may be eternal. Nothing here is conclusive for there is no grip by which this great creature can be seized as you might seize a drowning man by knotting your fist in his hair. Everything has gone to pieces, and not even the most pathetic striving can bring up more than an insufficient lock of hair. The peace that is on its way is not the fruit of a decision reached by man. It spreads apace like a gray leprosy.

Below me, those roads on which the caravan is breaking down, on which the enemy kills or quenches thirst at will, put me in mind of the miry regions where land and water are indistinguishable. This peace, that has become fused with this war, has begun to rot this war.

My friend Léon Werth heard on the road an extraordinary remark which he recorded in his excellent book. On the left were the Germans, and on the right the French. Between the two flowed the sluggish stream of refugees. Hundreds of women and children extricating themselves as well as they were able from flaming motorcars. A French artillery officer, entangled despite himself in the snarl, stopped to set up his Seventy-five beside the road. Opposite, the enemy aimed, missed his target, and mowed down the migrants in his line of fire. Whereupon Frenchwomen rushed upon the French lieutenant who, running with sweat, was stubbornly performing his incomprehensible duty, trying (with twelve men!) to hold a position that was untenable, and shouted at him:

"Go away! Go away! You cowards!"

The lieutenant and his men went away. Wherever they went, they were brought up against problems of peace, not of war. Of course children should not be massacred on the highways. Yet every soldier who pulled a trigger found a child in his line of fire. Every French lorry that moved or tried to move through that mob was potentially the cause of death among those people. For, moving upstream against the flow, the lorry could not but bottle up the whole highway.

"You are mad! Let us through! The children are dying!"

"We're fighting a war."

"What war? Where are you fighting it? It will take you three days to go a mile against this current."

Here was a handful of French soldiers in a lorry, trying to reach a point to which they had been ordered and which had certainly been abandoned to the enemy hours before. All that they could think about was their plain duty:

"Gangway, there!"

"Why don't you let us ride with you? You are beasts!"

A child bawls.

"And the kid. . . ."

But the kid has stopped crying. It takes milk to make a child cry.

"We're fighting a war."

There was a kind of despairing stupidity in the way they repeated it.

"But you will never find your war! You will croak on the road with the rest of us!"

"We're fighting a war."

They were by no means sure of what they were saying. They were by no means sure that they were fighting a war. They had never seen the enemy. They were rolling in a lorry towards a goal more fugitive than a mirage. They were moving towards nothing more than a peace that was a pool of putrefaction. And as they were caught up inextricably in the chaos, they jumped down from the lorry. Instantly they were surrounded.

"Have you any water?"

So they shared their water.

"Have you any bread?"

And they shared their bread.

"But you can't leave her here to die!"

So into their lorry they put the woman who lay dying in a car wrecked by the side of the road.

"And what about this child?"

The child went in beside the dying woman.

"And this woman in labor."

They put her in beside the living child.

And for another woman they found room merely because she was crying so bitterly.

It took an hour to free the lorry and turn it round till it too faced south. Rising like an erratic block, it too would now be carried downstream by the civilian flood. The soldiers had been converted to this peace. Because they hadn't been able to find the war. Because the musculature of the war was invisible. Because the gun aimed at you kills a child. Because on your way up to the lines you stumble upon women in labor. Because it is as useless to try to transmit information or receive a command as to communicate with the inhabitants of Mars. There is no longer an army. There are only men.

They have been converted to this peace. They have been changed by the force of things into mechanics, doctors, shepherds, stretcher-bearers. Because, since these little people are ignorant of how to cure the ills of their scrap-iron, the soldiers have taken to repairing their cars. And not one of them could tell you, in the midst of his sweating labour, whether he was a hero or a man who deserved to be court-martialled. It would not astonish him if he were decorated on the spot. Nor if he were stood up against a wall with a dozen bullets in his skull. Nor if he were demobilized. Nothing would astonish him. It is a long time since he and his kind have crossed the frontiers of astonishment.

Here is an immense stew in which not an order, not a movement, not a scrap of news, not a wave of anything at all can run on beyond a single mile. Exactly as the villages topple one by one into the common sewer, so these army lorries, absorbed into this peace, are one by one converted to this peace. These handfuls of men who would have accepted without question the notion of their imminent death—assuming they had so much as thought of it—now accept the duties they meet; and they fall to their job of repairing an antique carry-all into which three nuns, embarked upon God knows what pilgrimage, off for God knows what haven invented in a fairytale, have hustled a dozen children threatened by death.

XV

LIKE Alias when he slipped his gun back into its holster, I shall not sit in judgment upon these men who threw in their hand. Where was the breath to come from that would bring them life? Where the wave that would reach them, the vision that would unite them? All that they knew of the rest of the world was contained in the crazy rumors that sprouted by the roadside every mile or two in the form of ludicrous hypotheses, and somehow, slowly spreading through a mile or two of the chaos, were transformed into certainties. The United States had declared war. The Pope had committed suicide. Russian planes had set fire to Berlin. The Armistice had been signed three days ago. Hitler had landed in England.

There is no shepherd for the women and children, but none for the men, either. The general is able to communicate with his orderly. The cabinet minister with his

" . . . *three days earlier, I had seen the village in which we were billeted go to pieces.*"

(PAGE 119)

messenger. It may be that by their eloquence general and minister are able to transfigure their servants. Alias is able to communicate with his pilots and to win from them the sacrifice of their lives. The sergeant commanding the lorry is able to communicate with his squad. Beyond this, there is no way in the world of welding oneself to the rest. Even if we assume that at the moment of my flight towards Arras a genius existed who knew precisely what was happening in France, and that genius, that chief, had a plan that would save France, all that that chief possessed to carry out his plan was an electric cord which rang a bell in his reception room; and the army he commanded was made up of his messenger— provided that his messenger was still at his post in the reception room.

Those stray parties of soldiers who, separated from their scattered units, wandered over the jammed roads, were soldiers with no soldiering to do. But they were not filled with that despair which the vanquished patriot is supposed to feel. If in their confusion of mind they longed for peace, the peace they longed for meant to them the end of this unspeakable chaos and the return to some kind of identity, however humble. A shoemaker among them might dream that he was hammering pegs into a shoe. To hammer pegs into a shoe again would mean for him building a world. And if these men allowed themselves to be rolled back by the tide it was because the general chaos had disintegrated them, and not because they felt a horror of dying. They felt no horror of anything; they were empty of feeling.

We may take it as incontrovertible fact that men cannot be changed overnight from conquered into conquerors. Anybody who speaks of an army falling back in order to go on fighting is employing verbal subterfuge. The troops that fall back, and those that give battle, are not the same men. The army that fell back was no longer an army. I do not mean that men in retreat become unworthy of victory. Simply, the fact of falling back destroys all the ties, material and spiritual, by which they were once united. What was once an army becomes a scattering of disintegrated parts allowed to filter back to the rear. Fresh reserves are substituted for them, because the reserves constitute an organism, a whole. It is they, not a reorganized army, who undertake to block the path of the enemy. As for the fugitives, an attempt is made to collect them and re-shape them into an army. But where, as in France, there are no reserves to throw in, your initial retreat is irreparable.

There is but one principle of unity, and that is victory. Defeat not only splits men off from other men, it creates a split within the individual himself. If those apathetic fugitives do not mourn the fate of a collapsing France it is simply because they are the defeated. It is in the hearts of those men that France has been defeated. To weep for France is already the promise of victory.

Virtually none of those men, neither those still fighting nor those already benumbed, will see that whole, will see the face of a vanquished France, until later, when the tumult has died and silence has been restored. Today, in the midst of defeat, each man is concentrated upon a stubborn or shattered vulgar detail—a broken-down lorry, a road bottled up, a throttle stuck fast, a sortie that is a patent absurdity. The absurdity of the sortie is a sign of the collapse. The very act performed to arrest the collapse is a sign of absurdity. For every element stands divided against itself: there is no unity.

During a retreat there is no weeping over the universal disaster but only over the thing for which one is personally responsible. Alias, if he were to weep, would weep over the imbecility of the depots that refuse to deliver spare parts except against a requisition drawn in due form—parts which tomorrow will fall into the hands of the enemy. Collapsing France has become a deluge of fragments none of which has any identity—neither this aeroplane nor that lorry, neither that highway nor this foul throttle that refuses to budge.

Of course a collapse is a sad spectacle. Base men reveal themselves base. Pillagers reveal themselves pillagers. Institutions crumble. Troops heartsick and weary decompose. All these effects are implicit in defeat as death is implicit in the death rattle. But if the woman you loved were run over by a lorry, would you feel impelled to criticise her ugliness?

The injustice of defeat lies in the fact that its most

innocent victims are made to look like heartless accomplices. It is impossible to see behind defeat the sacrifices, the austere performance of duty, the self-discipline and the vigilance that are there—those things the god of battle does not take account of. Defeat cannot show love, though love is there. Defeat shows up generals without authority, men without organization, crowds that are passive. Unquestionably, slackers and cowards have their part in this defeat. But what do they signify? What is really significant is that the rumor of a Russian change of heart or an American intervention was enough to triple the value of those men. Enough to bind them together again in a common hope. Each time that such a rumor blew through France like a sea wind, our men were filled with a fresh exaltation. If France is to be judged, judge her not by the effects of her defeat but by her readiness to sacrifice herself.

In accepting the challenge of this war, France accepted the risk of disfigurement for a time by defeat. Was France to refuse this challenge, which is to say, this risk of disfigurement? There were Frenchmen who said: "We cannot in a single year create the forty million Frenchmen needed to match those eighty millions of Germans. We cannot overnight transform a nation of farmers into a people of factory workers such as the Germans are. We cannot change our wheatfields into coalfields. We cannot look for American intervention.

The Germans demand Danzig. They thus impose upon us, not the duty of saving Danzig, which is impossible, but of committing suicide in order to preserve our honor. Why? What dishonor is there in possessing a land that brings forth more wheat than machines? What dishonor is there in being only forty millions to the other man's eighty millions? Why should the dishonor be ours, and not the whole world's?" They were perfectly right. War, for France, signified disaster. Was France to refuse to fight in order to spare herself defeat? I think not. And France must instinctively have thought the same, since these warnings could not dissuade France from war. Among us, spirit conquered intelligence.

Life always bursts the boundaries of formulas. Defeat may prove to have been the only path to resurrection, despite its ugliness. I take it for granted that to create a tree I condemn a seed to rot. If the first act of resistance comes too late it is doomed to defeat. But it is, nevertheless, the awakening of resistance. Life may grow from it as from a seed.

France played her part. Her part consisted in offering herself up to be crushed and in seeing herself buried for a time in silence—since the world chose to arbitrate, and neither fought nor united against a common enemy. When a fort is to be taken by storm some men necessarily are in the front rank. Almost always, those men die. But the front rank must die if the fort is to be captured.

Since we of France agreed to fight this war without

illusions, this was the rôle that fell to us. We put farmers into the field against factory workers; one man into the field against three. And who is to sit in judgment upon the ugliness of the collapse? Is a pilot brought down in flames to be judged by the consequences? Obviously, he will be disfigured.

XVI

WHICH does not prevent this from being a funny war—aside from the spiritual reality that made it necessary. A funny war! I was never ashamed of this label. Hardly had we declared war when, being in no state to take the offensive, we began to look forward to our annihilation. Here it is.

We set up our haycocks against their tanks; and the haycocks turned out useless for defence. This day, as I fly to Arras, the annihilation has been consummated. There is no longer an army, there is no liaison, no matériel, and there are no reserves.

Nevertheless I carry on as solemnly as if this were war. I dive towards the German army at five hundred miles an hour. Why? I know! To frighten the Germans. To make them evacuate France. For since the intelligence I may bring back will be useless, this sortie can have no other purpose.

A funny war!

As a matter of fact, I am boasting. I have lost a great deal of altitude. Controls and throttles have thawed out. I have stepped down my speed to no more than three hundred and thirty miles an hour. A pity. I shall frighten the German army much less.

After all, it is we ourselves who call this a funny war. Why not? I should imagine that no one would deny us the right to call it that if we please, since it is we who are sacrificing ourselves, not those others who think our epithet immoral. Surely I have the right to joke about my death if joking about it gives me pleasure. And Dutertre has that right. I have the right to play with paradoxes. Why is it that those villages are still in flames? Why is it that that population has poured pell-mell out on the pavements? Why is it that we rush with inflexible determination towards an unmistakable slaughter-house?

I have every right to my joke; for in this moment I am fully conscious of what I am doing. I accept death. It is not danger that I accept. It is not combat that I accept. It is death. I have learnt a great truth. War is not the acceptance of danger. It is not the acceptance of combat. For the combatant, it is at certain moments the pure and simple acceptance of death.

And while men in the outside world were wondering, "Why is it that more Frenchmen are not being killed?" I was wondering, as I watched our crews go off to their death, "What are we giving ourselves to? Who is still paying this bill?"

For we were dying. For one hundred and fifty thousand Frenchmen were already dead in a single fortnight.
Those dead do not exemplify an extraordinary resistance. I am not singing the praises of an extraordinary resistance. Such a resistance was impossible. But there
were clusters of infantrymen still giving up their lives
in undefendable farmhouses. There were aviation crews
still melting like wax flung into a fire.

Look once again at Group 2-33. Will you explain to
me why, as I fly to Arras, we of Group 2-33 still agree
to die? For the esteem of the world? But esteem implies
the existence of a judge. And I have the impression that
none of us will grant whoever it may be the right to sit
in judgment. To us who imagine that we are defending
a cause which is fundamentally the common cause, the
cause of Poland, of Holland, of Belgium, of Norway; to
us who hold this view, the role of arbiter seems much
too comfortable. It is we who sit judgment upon the
arbiter. I invite you to try to explain to us who take off
with a "Very good, sir," having one chance in three to
get back when the sortie is an easy one; I invite you to
try to explain to a certain pilot out of another group,
half of whose neck and jaw were shot away so that he is
forced to renounce the love of woman for life, is frustrated in a fundamental right of man, frustrated as totally
as if he were behind prison walls, surrounded inescapa-
bly by his virtue and preserved totally by his disfigurement, isolated completely by his ugliness—I invite you
to explain to him that spectators are sitting in judgment

upon him. Toreadors live for the bull-fight crowd: we are not toreadors. If you said to another of my friends, to Hochedé, "You've got to go up because the crowd have their eye on you," Hochedé would answer: "There must be some mistake: it is I, Hochedé, who have my eye on the crowd."

For after all, why do we go on fighting? For democracy? If we die for democracy then we must be one of the democracies. Let the rest fight with us, if that is the case. But the most powerful of them, the only democracy that could save us, chooses to bide its time. Very good. That is its right. But by so doing, that democracy signifies that we are fighting for ourselves alone. And we go on fighting despite the assurance that we have lost the war. Why, then, do we go on dying? Out of despair? But there is no despair. You know nothing at all about defeat if you think there is room in it for despair.

There is a verity that is higher than the pronouncements of the intelligence. There is a thing which pierces and governs us and which cannot be grasped by the intelligence. A tree has no language. We are a tree. There are truths which are evident, thought not to be put into words. I do not die in order to obstruct the path of the invasion, for there is no shelter upon which I can fall back with those I love. I do not die to preserve my honor, since I deny that my honor is at stake, and I challenge the jurisdiction of my judge. Nor do I die out of desperation.

And yet Dutertre, looking at his map, having pinpointed the position of Arras somewhere round the one hundred and seventy-fifth degree of the compass, is about to say to me—I can feel it:

"175° captain."

And I shall accept.

XVII

"1 72°."

"Right! 172°."

Call it one seventy-two. Epitaph: "Maintained his course accurately on 172°." How long will this crazy challenge go on? I am flying now at two thousand three hundred feet beneath a ceiling of heavy clouds. If I were to rise a mere hundred feet Dutertre would be blind. Thus we are forced to remain visible to the anti-aircraft batteries and play the part of an archer's target for the Germans. Two thousand feet is a forbidden altitude. Your machine serves as a mark for the whole plain. You drain the cannonade of a whole army. You are within range of every calibre. You dwell an eternity in the field of fire of each successive weapon. You are not shot at with cannon but beaten with a stick. It is as if a thousand sticks were used to bring down a single walnut.

I had given a bit of thought to this problem. There is no question of a parachute. When the stricken plane dives to the ground the opening of the escape hatch takes more seconds than the dive of the plane allows. Opening the hatch involves seven turns of a crank that sticks. Besides, at full speed the hatch warps and refuses to slide.

That's that. The medicine had to be swallowed some day. I always knew it. Meanwhile, the formula is not complicated: stick to 172°. I was wrong to grow older. Pity. I was so happy as a child. I say so; but is it true? For already in that dim hall I was moving on this same course, 172°. Because of my uncles.

Now is the time when childhood seems sweet. Not only childhood, but the whole of my past life. I see it in perspective as if it were a landscape.

And it seems to me that I myself am unalterable. I have always felt what I now feel. Doubtless my joys and sadness changed object from time to time. But the feelings were always the same. I have been happy and unhappy. I have been punished and forgiven. I have worked well and badly. That depended on the days.

What is my earliest memory? I had a Tyrolian governess whose name was Paula. But she is not even a memory: she is the memory of a memory. Paula was already no more than a legend when at the age of five I sat marooned in the dim hall. Year after year my mother would say to us round the New Year, "There is a letter from Paula." That made all the children happy.

But why were we happy? None of us remembered Paula. She had gone back long before to her Tyrol. To her Tyrolian house. A house, we imagined, deep in snow and looking like the toy chalet on a Tyrolian barometer. And Paula, on sunny days, would come forth to stand in the doorway of that house like the mechanical doll over the Tyrolian barometer.

"Is Paula pretty?"

"Beautiful."

"Is it sunny in the Tyrol?"

"Always."

It was always fine weather in the Tyrol. The Tyrolian barometer sent Paula farther forward out of her doorway and on to her snow-covered lawn. Later, when I was able to write, I would be set to writing letters to Paula. They always began: "My dear Paula, I am very glad to be writing to you." The letters were a little like my prayers, for I did not know Paula.

"One seventy-four."

"Right! One seventy-four."

Call it one seventy-four. Must change that epitaph.

Strange, how of a sudden life has collected in a heap. I have packed up my memories. They will never be of use to me again. Nor to anyone else. I remember a great love. My mother would say to us: "Paula sends kisses to you all." And my mother would kiss us all for Paula.

"Does Paula know I am bigger?"

"Naturally."

Paula knew everything.

"Captain, they are beginning to fire."

Paula, they are firing at me! I glanced at the altimeter: two thousand one hundred and fifty feet. Clouds at two thousand three hundred. Well. Nothing to be done about it. What astonishes me is that beneath my cloudbank the world is not black, as I had thought it would be. It is blue. Marvellously blue. Twilight has come, and all the plain is blue. Here and there I see rain falling. Rain-blue.

"One sixty-eight."

"Right! One sixty-eight."

Call it one sixty-eight. Interesting, that the road to eternity should be zigzag. And so peaceful! The earth here looks like an orchard. A moment ago it seemed to me skeletal, inhumanly dessicated. But I am flying low in a sort of intimacy with it. There are trees, some standing isolated, others in clusters. You meet them. And green fields. And houses with red tile roofs and people out of doors. And lovely blue showers pouring all round them. The kind of weather in which Paula must have hustled us rapidly indoors.

"One seventy-five."

My epitaph has lost a good deal of its laconic dignity: "Maintained his course on 172°, 174°, 168°, 175°. . . ." I shall seem a very versatile fellow. What's that? Engine coughing? Growing cold. I shut the ventilators of the hood. Good. Time to change over to the reserve tanks. I pull the lever. Have I forgotten any-

" . . . *three nuns, embarked upon God knows what pilgrimage, off for God knows what haven.*" (PAGE 140)

thing? I glance at the oil gauge. Everything shipshape.

"Beginning to get a bit nasty, Captain."

Hear that, Paula? Beginning to get nasty. And yet I cannot help being astonished by the blue of the evening. It is so extraordinary. The color is so deep. And those fruit trees, plum trees, perhaps, flowing by. I am part of the countryside now. Gone are the museum cases. I am a marauder who has jumped over the wall. I am running through the wet alfalfa, stealing plums. This is a funny war, Paula. A war nostalgic and beautifully blue. I got lost somehow, and strayed into this strange country in my old age. . . . O, no, I am not frightened. It's a little melancholy, that's all.

"Zigzag, Captain!"

Here is a new game, Paula. You kick the rudder bar with your right foot and then your left, and the anti-aircraft battery can't touch you. When I fell down I used to bruise myself and raise swellings. I am sure you used to cure me with compresses of arnica. I am going to need arnica awfully, I think. But still, you know, this evening air is marvellously blue!

Forward of my plane I saw suddenly three lance-strokes aimed at my machine. Three long brilliant vertical twigs. The paths of tracer-bullets fired from a small-calibre gun. They were golden. Suddenly in the blue of the evening I had seen the spurting glow of a three-branched candlestick.

"Captain! Firing very fast to port. Hard down!"

I kicked my rudder.

"Getting worse!"

Worse?

Getting worse; but I am seated at the heart of the world. All my memories, all my needs, all my loves are now available to me. My childhood, lost in darkness like a root, is at my disposal. My life here begins with the nostalgia of a memory. Yes, it is getting worse; but I feel none of those things I thought I should feel when facing the claws of these shooting stars.

I am in a country that moves my heart. Day is dying. On the left I see great slabs of light among the showers. They are like panes in a cathedral window. Almost within reach, I can all but handle the good things of the earth. There are those plum trees with their plums. There is that earth-smelling earth. It must be wonderful to tramp over damp earth. You know, Paula, I am going gently forward, swaying to right and left like a loaded hay wain. You think an aeroplane moves fast; and indeed it does, if you think of it. But if you forget the machine, if you simply look on, why, you are merely taking a stroll in the country.

"Arras!"

Yes. Very far ahead. But Arras is not a town. Arras thus far is no more than a red plume against a blue background of night. Against a background of storm. For unmistakably, forward on the left, an awful squall is collecting. Twilight alone would not explain this half-light. It wants blocks of clouds to filter a glow so somber.

The flame of Arras is bigger now. You wouldn't call it the flame of a conflagration. A conflagration spreads like a chancre surrounded by no more than a narrow fringe of living flesh. That red plume permanently alight is the gleam of a lamp that might be smoking a bit. It is a flame without flicker, sure to last, well fed with oil. I can feel it moulded and kneaded out of a compact substance, something almost solid that the wind stirs from time to time and bends as it bends a tree. That's it: a tree. Arras is caught up in the mesh of roots of this tree. And all the pith of Arras, all the substance of Arras, all the treasures of Arras leap, now become sap, to nourish this tree.

I can see that occasionally top-heavy flame lose its equilibrium to right or left, belch forth an even blacker cloud of smoke, and then collect itself again. But I am still unable to make out the town.

The whole war is summed up in that glow. Dutertre says that it is getting worse. Perched up forward, he can see better than I can. Nevertheless, I am astonished by a sort of indulgence shown us: this venomous plain shoots forth few stars.

Yes, but. . . .

You remember, Paula, that in the fairy-tales of our childhood there was always a knight who passed through frightful experiences before reaching the enchanted castle. He scaled glaciers, leapt across abysses, outwitted villains. And in the end the castle rose before him out of a blue plain gentler beneath the galloping hoofs than a green lawn. Already he thought himself victorious. Ah, Paula, you can't fool an old fairy-tale reader! The worst of his trials was still before him—the ogre, the dragon, the guardian of the castle.

Like that knight, I ride in the blue of the evening towards my castle of flame. And not for the first time. You had already left us when we began to play games. You missed the game called Aklin the Knight. We had invented it ourselves, for we sneered at games that other children could play. This one was played out of doors in stormy weather when, after the first flashes of lightning, we could tell from the rising smell of the earth and the sudden quivering of the leaves that the cloud was about to burst. There was a moment when the thickness in the boughs turned into a lightly sough- ing moss. That was the signal. Nothing could hold us back.

We would run as fast as we could from the deep end of the park towards the house, flying breathlessly across the lawns. The first drops of that rain were always scat- tered and heavy. The child first touched by them was beaten. Then the next. Then the third. Then the rest. He who survived longest was acknowledged the darling of the gods, the invulnerable. Until the next storm came he had the right to call himself Aklin the Knight. It was only a matter of seconds, and the result was each time a hecatomb of children.

I fly my plane, playing at being Aklin the Knight. I

am running slowly and out of breath towards my castle of flame.

"Captain! Captain! I've never seen anything like it!"

Nor have I.

Where now is my vulnerability? Unknown to myself, I had been hoping. . . .

XVIII

DESPITE my lack of altitude, I had been hoping. Despite the tank parks, despite the flame over Arras. Desperately, I had been hoping. I had escaped into a memory of early childhood in order to recapture the sense of sovereign protection. For man there is no protection. Once you are a man you are left to yourself. But who can avail against a little boy whose hand is firmly clasped in the hand of an all-powerful Paula? Paula, I have used thy shade as a shield.

I have used every trick in my bag. When Dutertre said to me, "It's getting worse," I used even that threat as a source of hope. We were at war: necessarily, then, there had to be evidence of war. The evidence was no more than a few streaks of light. "Is this your terrible danger of death over Arras? Don't make me laugh!"

The man condemned had imagined that the executioner would look like a pallid robot. Arrives a quite

ordinary decent-appearing fellow who is able to sneeze,
even to smile. The man condemned clings to that smile
as to a promise of reprieve. The promise is a wraith. The
headsman sneezes—and the head falls nevertheless. But
who can reject hope?

I myself could not but be deceived by the smile I saw
—since this whole world was snug and verdant, since the
wet slate and tile shone so cordially, since from minute
to minute nothing changed nor promised to change.
Since we three, Dutertre, the gunner, and I, were men
walking across fields, sauntering idly home without so
much as the need to raise our collars, so little was it
raining. Since here at the heart of the German zone
nothing stood forth that was really worth telling about,
whence it must follow that farther on the war need not
of necessity be different to this. Since it seemed that the
enemy had scattered and melted into the wide and rural
plain, standing perhaps at the rate of one soldier to a
house, one soldier to a tree, one of whom, remembering
now and then the war, would fire. The order had been
drummed into the fellow's ears: "Fire on all enemy
planes." But he had been daydreaming, and the order
had been dimmed by the dream. He let fly his three
rounds without much expectation of results. Thus at
dusk I used to shoot ducks that meant very little to me
if the evening invited my soul. I would fire while talking about something else. It hardly disturbed the ducks.

It is so easy to spin fine tales to oneself. The enemy takes
aim, but without firm purpose; and he misses me. Others

in turn let us pass. Those who might trip us up are per-haps at this moment inhaling with pleasure the smell of the night, or lighting cigarettes, or finishing a funny story—and they let us pass. Still others, in the village where they are billeted, are perhaps dipping their tin cups into the soup. A roar rises and dies away. Friend or enemy? There isn't time for them to find out: their eyes are on the cup now filling—they let us pass. And I, whistling a tune and my hands in my pockets, do my best to walk as casually as I can through this garden forbidden to trespassers where every guard, counting on the next guard, lets us pass.

How vulnerable I was! Yet it seemed to me that my very vulnerability was a trap, a means of cajoling them: "Why fire? Your friends are sure to bring me down a little farther on." And they would shrug their shoul-ders: "Go break your neck somewhere else." They were leaving the chore to the next battery—because they were anxious not to miss their turn at the soup, were finishing their funny story, or were simply enjoying the evening breeze. I was taking advantage of their negli-gence, and I was saved by the seeming coincidence that all of them at once appeared to be weary of war. And why not? Already I was thinking vaguely that from sol-dier to soldier, squad to squad, village to village, I should get through this sortie. After all, what were we but a passing plane in the evening sky? Not enough to make a man raise his eyes.

Of course I hoped to get back. But I could feel at the

same time that something was in the air. You are sentenced: a penalty hangs over you; but the gaol in which you are locked up continues silent. You cling to that silence. Every second that drops is like the one that went before. There is no reason why the second about to drop should change the world. Such a task is too heavy for a single second. Each second that follows safeguards your silence. Already this silence seems perpetual.

But the step of him who must come sounds in the corridor.

Something in this countryside suddenly exploded. So a log that seemed burnt out crackles suddenly and shoots forth its sparks. How did it happen that the whole plain started up at the same moment? When spring comes, all the trees at once drop their seed. Why this sudden springtime of arms? Why this luminous flood rising towards us and, of a sudden, universal?

My first feeling was that I had been careless. I had ruined everything. A wink, a single gesture is enough to topple you from the tight-rope. A mountain climber coughs, and he releases an avalanche. Once he has released the avalanche, all is over.

We had been swaying heavily through this blue swamp already drowned in night. We had stirred up this silent slime; and now, in tens of thousands, it was sending towards us its golden bubbles. A nation of jugglers had burst into dance. A nation of jugglers was dribbling its projectiles in tens of thousands in our direction. Because they came straight at us, at first they appeared to be motionless. Like colored balls which jugglers seem not so much to fling into the air as to release upwards, they rose in a lingering ascension. I could see those tears of light flowing towards me through a silence as of oil. That silence in which jugglers perform.

Each burst of a machine gun or a rapid-fire cannon shot forth hundreds of these phosphorescent bullets that followed one another like the beads of a rosary. A thousand elastic rosaries strung themselves out towards the plane, drew themselves out to the breaking point, and burst at our height. When, missing us, the string went off at a tangent, its speed was dizzying. The bullets were transformed into lightning. And I flew drowned in a crop of trajectories as golden as stalks of wheat. I flew at the center of a thicket of lance strokes. I flew threatened by a vast and dizzying flutter of knitting needles. All the plain was now bound to me, woven and wound round me, a coruscating web of golden wire.

I leant towards the earth and saw those storied levels of luminous bubbles rising with the tardy movement of veils of fog. I saw as I stared the slow vortex of seed, swirling like the husks of threshed grain. And when I raised my head I saw on the horizon those stacks of lances. Guns firing? Not at all! I am attacked by cold steel. These are swords of light. I feel . . . certainly not in danger! Dazzled I am by the luxury that envelopes me.

What's that!

I was jolted nearly a foot out of my seat. The plane has been rammed hard; I thought. It has burst, been ground to bits. . . . But it hasn't; it hasn't. . . . I can still feel it responsive to the controls. This was but the first blow of a deluge of blows. Yet there was no sign of explosion below. The smoke of the heavy guns had probably blended into the dark ground.

I raised my head and stared. What I saw was without appeal.

XIX

I HAD been looking on at a carnival of light. The ceiling had risen little by little and I had been unaware of an intervening space between the clouds and me. I had been zigzagging along a line of flight dotted by ground batteries. Their tracer bullets had been spraying the air with wheat-colored shafts of light. I had forgotten that at the top of their flight the shells of those batteries must burst. And now, raising my head, I saw around and before me those rivets of smoke and steel driven into the sky in the pattern of towering pyramids.

I was quite aware that those rivets were no sooner driven than all danger went out of them, that each of those puffs possessed the power of life and death only for a fraction of a second. But so sudden and simultaneous was their appearance that the image flashed into my mind of conspirators intent upon my death. Abruptly their purpose was revealed to me, and I felt on the nape of my neck the weight of an inescapable reprobation.

Muffled as those explosions reached me, their sound covered by the roar of my engines, I had the illusion of an extraordinary silence. Those vast packets of smoke and steel moving soundlessly upward and behind me with the lingering flow of icebergs, persuaded me that, seen in their perspective, I must be virtually motionless. I was motionless in the dock before an immense assizes. The judges were deliberating my fate, and there was nothing I could plead. Once again the timelessness of suspense seized me. I thought,—I was still able to think, —"They are aiming too high," and I looked up in time to see straight overhead, swinging away from me as if with reluctance, a swarm of black flakes that glided like eagles. Those eagles had given me up. I was not to be their prey. But even so, what hope was there for me?

The batteries that continued to miss me continued also to readjust their aim. New walls of smoke and steel continued to be built up round me as I flew. The ground-fire was not seeking me out, it was closing me in.

"Dutertre! How much more of this is there?"

"Stick it out three minutes, Captain. Looks bad, though."

"Think we'll get through?"

"Not on your life!"

There never was such muck as this murky smoke, this mess as grimy as a heap of filthy rags. The plain was blue. Immensely blue. Deep-sea blue.

What was a man's life worth between this blue plain and this foul sky? Ten seconds, perhaps; or twenty. The shock of the exploding shells set all the sky shuddering. When a shell burst very near, the explosion rumbled along the plane like rock dropping through a chute. And when for a moment the roar stopped, the plane rang with a sound that was almost musical. Like a sigh, almost; and the sigh told us that the plane had been missed. Those bursts were like the thunder: the closer they came, the simpler they were. A rumble meant distance, a clean *bang!* meant that we had been squarely hit by a shell fragment. The tiger does not do a messy job on the ox it brings down. The tiger sets its claws into the ox without skidding. It takes possession of the ox. Each square hit by a fragment of shell sank into the hull of the plane like a claw into living flesh.

"Anybody hurt?"

"Not I!"

"Gunner! You all right?"

"O.K., sir!"

Somehow those explosions, though I find I must mention them, did not really count. They drummed upon the hull of the plane as upon a drum. They pierced my fuel tanks. They might as easily have drummed upon our bellies, pierced them instead. What is the belly but a kind of drum? But who cares what happens to his body? Extraordinary, how little the body matters.

There are things that we might learn about our bodies in the course of everyday living if we were not blind to patent evidence. It takes this rain of upsurging streamers of light, this assault by an army of lances, this assizes set up for the last judgment, to teach us those things.

I used to wonder as I was dressing for a sortie what a man's last moments were like. And each time, life would give the lie to the ghosts I evoked. Here I was, now, naked and running the gauntlet, unable so much as to guard my head by arm or shoulder from the crazy blows raining down upon me. I had always assumed that the ordeal, when it came, would be an ordeal that concerned my flesh. My flesh alone, I assumed, would be subjected to the ordeal. It was unavoidable that in thinking of these things I should adopt the point of view of my body. Like all men, I had given it a good deal of time. I had dressed it, bathed it, fed it, quenched its thirst. I had identified myself with this domesticated animal. I had taken it to the tailor, the surgeon, the barber. I had been unhappy with it, cried out in pain with it, loved with it. I had said of it, "This is me." And now of a sudden my illusion vanished. What was my body to me? A kind of flunkey in my service. Let but my anger wax hot, my love grow exalted, my hatred collect in me, and that boasted solidarity between me and my body was gone.

Your son is in a burning house. Nobody can hold you back. You may burn up; but do you think of that? You are ready to bequeath the rags of your body to any man

"*We set up our haycocks against their tanks; and the haycocks turned out useless for defense.*"

(PAGE 151)

who will take them. You discover that what you set so much store by is trash. You would sell your hand, if need be, to give a hand to a friend. It is in your act that you exist, not in your body. Your act is yourself, and there is no other you. Your body belongs to you: it is not you. Are you about to strike an enemy? No threat of bodily harm can hold you back. You? It is the death of your enemy that is you. You? It is the rescue of your child that is you. In that moment you exchange yourself against something else; and you have no feeling that you lost by the exchange. Your members? Tools. A tool snaps in your hand: how important is that tool? You exchange yourself against the death of your enemy, the rescue of your child, the recovery of your patient, the perfection of your theorem. Here is a pilot of my Group wounded and dying. A true citation in general orders would read: "Called out to his observer, 'They've got me! Beat it! And for God's sake don't lose those notes!'" What matters is the notes, the child, the patient, the theorem. Your true significance becomes dazzlingly evident. Your true name is duty, hatred, love, child, theorem. There is no other you than this.

The flames of the house, of the diving plane, strip away the flesh; but they strip away the worship of the flesh too. Man ceases to be concerned with himself: he recognizes of a sudden what he forms part of. If he should die, he would not be cutting himself off from his kind, but making himself one with them. He would not be losing himself, but finding himself. This that I affirm is not the wishful thinking of a moralist. It is an every-day fact. It is a commonplace truth. But a fact and a truth hidden under the veneer of our everyday illusion. Dressing and fretting over the fate that might befall my body, it was impossible for me to see that I was fretting over something absurd. But in the instant when you are giving up your body, you learn to your amazement—all men always learn to their amazement—how little store you set by your body. It would be foolish to deny that during all those years of my life when nothing insistent was prompting me, when the meaning of my existence was not at stake, it was impossible for me to conceive that anything might be half so important as my body. But here in this plane I say to my body (in effect), "I don't care a button what becomes of you. I have been expelled out of you. There is no hope of your surviving this, and yet I lack for nothing. I reject all that I have been up to this very instant. For in the past it was not I who thought, not I who felt: it was you, my body. One way and another, I have dragged you through life to this point; and here I discover that you are of no importance."

Already at the age of fifteen I might have learnt this lesson. I had a younger brother who lay dying. One morning towards four o'clock his nurse woke me and said that he was asking for me.

"Is he in pain?" I asked.

The nurse said nothing, and I dressed as fast as I could.

When I came into his room he said to me in a matter-of-fact voice, "I wanted to see you before I died. I am going to die." And with that he stiffened and winced and could not go on. Lying in pain, he waved his hand as if saying "No!" I did not understand. I thought it was death he was rejecting. The pain passed, and he spoke again. "Don't worry," he said. "I'm all right. I can't help it. It's my body." His body was already foreign territory, something not himself.

He was very serious, this younger brother who was to die in twenty minutes. He had called me in because he felt a pressing need to hand on part of himself to me. "I want to make my will," he said; and he blushed with pride and embarrassment to be talking like a grown man. Had he been a builder of towers he would have bequeathed to me the finishing of his tower. Had he been a father, I should have inherited the education of his children. A reconnaissance pilot, he would have passed on to me the intelligence he had gleaned. But he was a child, and what he confided to my care was a toy steam engine, a bicycle, and a rifle.

Man does not die. Man imagines that it is death he fears; but what he fears is the unforeseen, the explosion. What man fears is himself, not death. There is no death when you meet death. When the body sinks into death, the essence of man is revealed. Man is a knot, a web, a mesh into which relationships are tied. Only those relationships matter. The body is an old crock that nobody will miss. I have never known a man to think of himself when dying. Never.

"Captain!"

"What's up?"

"Getting hot!"

"Gunner!"

"Er . . . yes, sir."

"What—."

My question vanished in the shock of another explosion.

"Dutertre!"

"Captain?"

"Hurt?"

"No."

"You, gunner!"

"Yes, sir."

"I wa—."

I seemed to be running the plane into a bronze wall. A voice in my ear said, "Boy! oh, boy!" as I looked up to measure the distance to the overhanging clouds. The sharper the angle at which I stared, the more densely the murky tufts seemed to be piled up. Seen straight overhead, the sky was visible between them, and they hung curved and scattered, forming a gigantic coronet in the air.

A man's thigh muscles are incredibly powerful. I bore down upon the rudder bar with all my strength

and sent the plane shuddering and skidding at right
angles to our line of flight. The coronet swung overhead and slid down on my right. I had got away from
one of the batteries and left it firing wasted packets
of shell. But before I could bring my other thigh into
play the ground battery had set straight what hung
askew—the coronet of smoke was back again. Once more
I bore down, and again the plane groaned and swayed
in this swampy sky. All the weight of my body was
on that bar, and the machine had swung, had skidded
squarely to starboard. The coronet curved now above
me on the left.

Would we last it out? But how could we! Each time
that I brought the ship brutally round, the deluge of
lance-strokes followed me before I could jerk back
again. Each time the coronet was set back into place and
the shell bursts shook up the plane anew. And each time,
when I looked down, I saw again that same dizzyingly
slow ascension of golden bubbles that seemed to be
accurately centered upon my plane. How did it happen
that we were still whole? I began to believe in us. "I am
invulnerable, after all," I said to myself, "I am winning. From second to second, I am more and more the
winner."

"Anybody hurt yet?"

"Nobody."

They were unhurt. They were invulnerable. They
were victorious. I was the owner of a winning team.
And from that moment each explosion seemed to me

not to threaten us but to temper us. Each time, for a fraction of a second, it seemed to me that my plane had been blown to bits; but each time it responded anew to the controls and I nursed it along like a coachman pulling hard on the reins. I began to relax, and a wave of jubilation went through me. There was just time enough for me to feel fear as no more than a physical stiffening induced by a loud crash, when instantly after each buffet a wave of relief went through me. I ought to have felt successively the shock, then the fear, then the relief; but there wasn't time. What I felt was the shock, then instantly the relief. Shock, relief. Fear, the intermediate step, was missing. And during the second that followed the shock I did not live in the expectancy of death in the second to come, but in the conviction of resurrection born of the second just passed. I lived in a sort of slipstream of joy, in the wake of my jubilation. A prodigiously unlooked-for pleasure was flowing through me. It was as if, with each second that passed, life was being granted me anew. As if with each second that passed my life became a thing more vivid to me. I was living. I was alive. I was still alive. I was the source of life itself. I was thrilled through with the intoxication of living. "The heat of battle" is a familiar phrase; the heat of living is a truer one. "I wonder," I said to myself, "if those Germans below who are firing at us know that they are creating life within us?"

All my tanks had been pierced, both gas and oil. Otherwise we seemed to be sound. Dutertre called out that he was through, and once again I looked up and calculated the distance to the clouds. I raised the nose of the ship, and once again I sent the plane zigzagging as I climbed. Once again I cast a glance earthwards. What I saw I shall not forget. The plain was crackling everywhere with short wicks of spurting flame—the rapid-fire cannon. The colored balls were still floating upward through an immense blue aquarium of air. Arras was glowing dark red like iron on the anvil, a flame fed by subterranean stores, by the sweat of men, the inventions of men, the arts of men, the memories and patrimony of men, all these braided in the ruddy ascension of that single plume that changed them into fire and ash, borne away on the wind.

Already I was flying through the first packets of mist. Golden arrows still rose and pierced the belly of the cloud, and just as the cloud closed round me I caught through an opening my last glimpse of that scene. For a single instant the flame over Arras rose up glowing in the night like a lamp in the nave of a cathedral. The lamp that was Arras was burning in the service of a cult, but at a price. By to-morrow it would have consumed Arras and itself have been consumed.

"Everything all right, Dutertre?"

"First rate, Captain. Two-forty, please. We shan't be able to come down out of this cloud for about twenty minutes. Then I'll pick up a landmark along the Seine somewhere."

"Everything all right, gunner?"

"Everything fine, sir."

"Not too hot for you, was it?"

"No, I guess not, sir."

Hard for him to tell. But he was feeling fine. I thought of Gavoille's gunner. In the days when this was still a very odd war, we used to do long-distance reconnaissance over Germany. There was a night over the Rhine when eighty searchlights picked up Gavoille's plane and built a giant basilica round it. The anti-aircraft began to fire, and suddenly Gavoille heard his gunner talking to himself—for the inter-com is hardly a private line. The man was muttering a dialogue of one: "Think you've been around, do you? I'll tell you something you've never seen!" He was feeling fine, that gunner.

I flew on, drawing deep slow breaths. I filled my lungs to the bottom. It was wonderful to breathe again. There were many things I was going to find out about. First I thought of Alias. No, that's not true. I thought first of my host, my farmer. I still looked forward to asking him how many instruments he thought a pilot had to watch. Sorry, but I am stubborn about some things. One hundred and three. He would never guess. Which reminds me. When your tanks have been pierced, it does no harm to have a look at your gauges. Wonderful tanks! Their rubber coatings had done their job; automatically, they had contracted and plugged the

holes made by bullets and shell splinters. I had a look at
my stabilizers too. This cloud we flew in was a storm
cloud. It shook us up pretty badly.

"Think we can come down now?"

"Ten minutes more. Better wait another ten minutes."

Of course I could wait another ten minutes. . . .
Yes, I had thought of Alias. Was he still expecting us,
I wondered? The other day we had been half an hour
late. A half hour is generally longer than you ought to
be: it means trouble. I had landed and run to join the
Group, who were at table. I had opened the door and
fallen into a chair beside Alias. At that moment he had
a cluster of spaghetti on his fork and was preparing to
tuck it away. He jumped, took a good look at me, and
sat perfectly still, the noodles hanging from his fork.

"Well, I . . . Glad to see you," he said.

And he stuffed the noodles into his mouth.

The major has one serious fault, to my mind. He
insists stubbornly on examining his pilots about their
sorties. He will examine me. He will sit looking at me
with embarrassing patience, waiting for me to spin out
my commonplace observations. He will have armed
himself with paper and pencil, determined not to lose a
single drop of the elixir I shall presumably have brought
back.

I thought of school: "Saint-Exupéry, how do you
integrate Bernoulli's equations?"

"Er . . . er."

Bernoulli, Bernoulli. Let me see. . . . And you stiffened under the teacher's gaze, motionless, fixed in place like an insect on a pin.

Intelligence is Dutertre's business, not mine. He is the observer; I am the pilot. From where he sits he can see straight below. He sees lots of things—lorries, barges, tanks, soldiers, cannon, horses, railway stations, trains, station masters. From where I sit I see the world at an angle. I see clouds, sea, rivers, mountains, sun. I see roughly, and get only a general impression.

"Major, you know as well as I do that a pilot . . ."

"Come, come, Saint-Ex! You do see some things, after all."

I . . . Oh, yes! Flames. Villages burning. Doesn't the major think that interesting?

"Nonsense! The whole country is on fire. What else?"

Why must Alias be so cruel?

XX

W HAT I bring back from this sortie is not matter for a report. When Alias examines me I shall flunk like a schoolboy standing before all the class at a blackboard. I shall seem very unhappy, and yet I shall not be unhappy. Unhappiness is behind me. It fled in that instant when the shell bursts began to drum upon the plane. Had I turned back one second before, I should have missed knowing myself.

I should never have known the flood of affection that at this moment fills my heart. I am going back to my own kind. I am going home. I am like a housewife whose shopping is done and who is on her way home, her mind on the savoury dinner with which she is about to delight her family. Her market basket swings on her arm to left and right. From time to time she raises the newspaper that covers it, and peers in. Everything is there: nothing has been forgotten. She smiles to herself at the thought of the surprise she is planning. She lingers a little, glances into the shop windows.

I too should be glancing into my shop windows if Dutertre did not insist that I go on in this pallid prison of cloud. I should be glancing at the passing country-side. Though Dutertre is right to insist that I be patient. This area over which I fly is treacherous: its air is heavy with conspiracy. Each little manor house below, with its slightly ridiculous lawn and handful of domesticated trees standing like an artless background for a family photograph, has become a blind. If I were to fly low over those houses, no friendly hands would wave to me, but shells would rise and explode.

Yet even in the belly of this cloud I am on my way home from market. The major was right, after all. When he sent us off in a voice that seemed to say, "And then you take the first turn to the right, where you will see a tobacco shop," his voice was pitched on the right note. My conscience is at rest. I have the major's matches in my pocket—or more truly, Dutertre has them in his pocket. How Dutertre manages to re-member what he saw, I cannot imagine. But that is his business. My mind is on more serious things. We shall land; and if the enemy spare us the nuisance of a sudden rush to still another field, I shall challenge Lacordaire and beat him at chess. He hates to lose. So do I. But I shall win.

Yesterday, be it said without dishonour, Lacordaire got tight. At least, a little tight. He had got tight in order to console himself. Coming in from a sortie, he had forgotten to release his landing gear and had set the plane down on her belly. Unfortunately, Alias had seen him do it; but he had not said a word. And Lacordaire, a pilot of long experience, had stood by, waiting for Alias to turn upon him. He had stood by hoping that Alias would curse him. A violent tongue lashing would have done him good. It would have allowed him to explode too. It would have allowed him to get off his chest the rage against himself that was swelling in him. But Alias had merely shaken his head sadly. Alias' mind was on the plane, not on the pilot. To the major, this accident was a kind of anonymous misfortune, a statistical tax levied on the Group. It was the effect of one of those moments of absentmindedness that attack even the most experienced pilots. It was an injustice, and Lacordaire was its victim. Except this blunder, Lacordaire's professional record was clean. Alias knew this, and all that bothered him was the plane. Automatically, without thinking, he turned to Lacordaire and asked him how bad he thought the damage was. And I could feel Lacordaire's pent up rage rise a degree at the question. You put your hand cordially on the torturer's shoulder and say to him, "How badly do you think your victim is suffering?" Truly, the human heart is unfathomable. That friendly hand soliciting the torturer's sympathy exasperates the torturer. He flings a black look at the victim and is sorry he hasn't finished her off.

I am on my way home. Group 2-33 is my home. And I understand the men who live in my home. I cannot be mistaken about Lacordaire. Lacordaire cannot be mistaken about me. Nothing is stronger than the community of feeling between us, the feeling that goes through me when I say, "We of Group 2-33." The particles, the fragments that we are, collect and possess meaning in the fact of the Group.

Flying in the cloud, I think of Gavoille and Hochedé. I am stirred by the community of feeling that binds me to them. I wonder about Gavoille. What sort of people does he come of? There is a wonderful earthy substance in Gavoille. A memory sweeps suddenly over me and fills me with warmth. At Orconte, Gavoille too was billeted with a peasant. One day he said to me, "The farmer's wife killed a pig the other day. She wants us to try her blood-sausage."

Three of us sat eating the wonderful black and crackling skin—Gavoille, Israel, and I. There was a crock of white wine to wash it down. Gavoille said as we ate, "I bought this for the farmer's wife, thinking she'd like it. Write something in it for her." It was a copy of one of my books. I was not in the least embarrassed. I wrote in it with pleasure, to please them both. Gavoille sat scratching his leg. Israel was stuffing his pipe. The farmer's wife seemed pleased to have a book inscribed by an author. The kitchen was redolent of the sausage. I was a little tight, for the white wine was heady. I did not feel in the least strange, despite the fact of inscribing a book—a thing which in other circumstances has always bothered me. I did not feel at all out of place. Despite the book, I did not think of myself either as an author or as an outsider. I was not an outsider. Israel looked on and smiled pleasantly as I wrote my name. Gavoille went on scratching his leg. And I felt grateful for the way they took it. That book might have made them look upon me as an outsider. Yet it didn't. I was still one of them.

The notion of looking on at life has always been hateful to me. What am I if I am not a participant? In order to be, I must participate. I am fed by the quality that resides in those who participate with me. That quality is something the men of the Group never think of—not out of humility, but because they do not stoop to measure it. Gavoille does not wonder about himself, nor does Israel. Each of these men is a web woven of his job, his trade, his duty. That smoking sausage, eaten in these circumstances, is woven into that web. The presence of these men is dense, full of meaning, and it warms my heart. I am able to sit with them in silence. To drink my white wine with them. To sign my book without thereby cutting myself off from them. Nothing in the world is strong enough to wreck this fellowship.

I do not mean to belittle the workings of the mind or the products of the intelligence. I admire a limpid intelligence as much as any man. But what is a man if he lacks substance? If he is a mere intellect and not a being?

"Something in this countryside suddenly exploded." (PAGE 171)

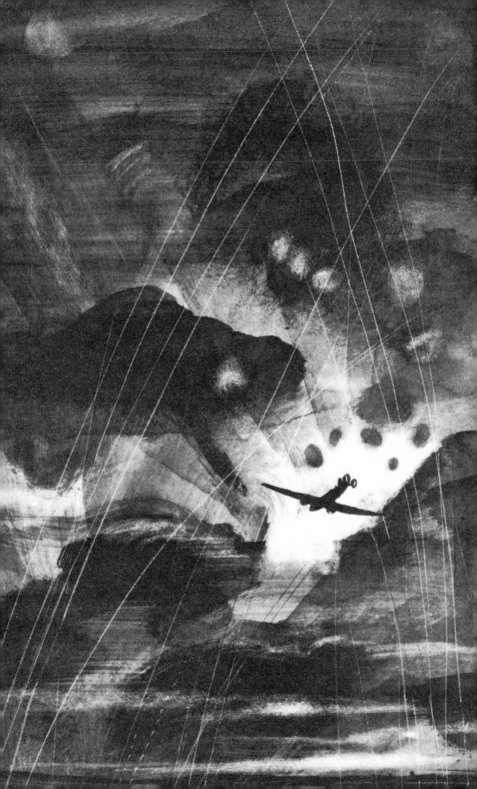

As formerly I saw substance in Guillaumet, so now I see it in Gavoille, in Israel.

I have mentioned before that because I was a writer I might have enjoyed certain advantages, certain liberties in this war. I might for example have been free to leave Group 2-33 the day I no longer approved of what I was ordered to do. But that kind of liberty I reject almost with terror. It is no more than the liberty to be a by-stander, which is to say the liberty not to exist. There is no growth except in the fulfillment of obligations.

We in France all but died of intelligence unsupported by substance. Gavoille exists. He loves, hates, rejoices, complains. He is shaped and heightened by the strands woven together and constituting his being. And exactly as, sitting with him at table, I took pleasure from the crisp sausage we shared, so I take pleasure from the obligations of the craft that fuse us of the Group into a common being. I love Group 2-33. I do not love it with the love of a spectator looking on at a handsome spectacle. I don't give a button for spectacles. I love Group 2-33 because I am part of it and it is part of me, because it nourishes me and I contribute to nourishing it.

And now, flying home from Arras, I am more than ever interwoven with Group 2-33. I have formed still another tie with it. I have intensified in me that feeling of communion with it that is to be relished and left unspoken. Each of us had risked his life in more or less the same fashion. Israel had disappeared. It seemed pretty certain that in the course of to-day's outing I too should disappear. What have I earned by this swing round the sky except a slightly better right to sit down at their table and be silent with them? The right is dearly bought; but it is a dear right. It is the right to be, and thus to escape non-being.

Yet the notion that I shall stammer when, some minutes from now, Alias will put his questions, makes me go red. I shall feel ashamed, I know. The major will think me a little idiotic. The shame that I feel already by anticipation is genuine. Yet . . . Once again I had taken off—this time to Arras—in search of the proof of my good faith. I had risked my flesh in this sortie. I had risked it being pretty sure that I should lose it. I had given everything to the rules of the game in order to turn them somehow into something other than the rules of the game. And this being so, I have won the right to appear sheepish when the major examines me. The right, that is, to participate. To be interwoven with the rest. To commune with them. To give and receive. To be more than myself. To possess this plenitude that swells so powerfully within me. To feel the love that I feel for the Group, a love that is not an impulse from without but is something inward and never to be manifested— except at a farewell dinner. At a farewell dinner you are sure to be a little drunk, and the benevolence born of alcohol is sure to make you lean towards your friends as a tree whose boughs bend with gifts. My love of the Group has no need of definition. It is woven of bonds.

It is my substance. I am of the Group, and the Group is of me.

And as I think of the Group, it is impossible for me not to think of Hochedé. Hochedé made a total gift of himself to this war. More, probably, than any of us, Hochedé dwells permanently in that state which I have striven so hard to attain to. Hochedé has arrived at the goal towards which the rest of us tend, the goal I seek to reach.

Hochedé is a former sergeant recently promoted second lieutenant. I can imagine that his culture is slight. He is unable to shed any light upon himself. But he is constructed, he is complete. The word duty loses all bombast when applied to Hochedé. Any man would be happy to accept his duty as Hochedé does. When I think of Hochedé, I reproach myself all my petty renunciations, my negligences, my laziness, and my moments of intellectualism, which is to say scepticism. This is not a sign in me of virtue but of intelligent jealousy. I should like to exist as completely as Hochedé does. A tree solidly planted on its roots is a beautiful thing. The permanence of Hochedé is a beautiful thing. Hochedé could never disappoint.

Volunteer? We were all volunteers on all our sorties. For the rest of us, the reason was a vague need to believe in ourselves. By volunteering, we outdid ourselves a little. Hochedé was a volunteer by nature. He was, in essence, this war. The fact was so evident that when a plane was bound to be sacrificed the major thought

automatically of Hochedé. "Look here, Hochedé. . . ."
Hochedé was steeped in this war as a monk is steeped in
religion. For whom did he fight? For himself, since he
was interwoven with the war, with the Group, with
France. Hochedé was fused together with a certain substance, and that substance, which was his own significance, had to be saved. At Hochedé's level, life and
death are somewhat the same thing. Hochedé was already part of both. Perhaps without realizing it, he
hardly feared death. Stick it out; make others stick it
out—that was what mattered. For Hochedé, life and
death had become reconciled.

The first time that Hochedé amazed me was when, he
being still a sergeant, Gavoille tried to borrow his stop-
watch in order to clock a ship.

"Lieutenant, sir. I. . . . I'd rather not lend it."

"Don't be a fool! I'll give it back to you in ten minutes."

"Sir, there's a stop-watch at the squadron depot."

"Yes, a broken one. I know it."

"Sir, I . . . Nobody lends stop-watches, sir. I don't
have to lend it to the lieutenant. It's not in orders. The
lieutenant hasn't the right to insist."

Military discipline and respect for the hierarchy may
demand that a Hochedé just unlimbered from a parachute and out of a burning plane jump instantly into another plane and take off on a sortie twice as dangerous.
It may not demand that he turn over to an officer a
stop-watch that has cost him three months' pay and that

seems to him as precious and fragile as a baby. You can tell by the way some men wave their arms that they have no respect for stop-watches. Gavoille seemed to Hochedé just such a man. And when Hochedé, still fuming with indignation, but having won out, left the room with his stop-watch over his heart, I could have embraced him. Hochedé was a man with a heart. He would fight to the death for his stop-watch. His stop-watch existed. He would die for his country. His country existed. Hochedé existed, being interwoven with both. He was shaped and heightened by his ties with watch and country.

And so Hochedé was precious in my eyes, though there was no need to tell him so. For like reasons, when Guillaumet, the best friend I ever had, was killed in the course of duty, there was no need for me to speak of him. We had flown the same airlines. Participated in the building of the same structures. Were of the same substance. Something of me died in him. Guillaumet became one of the companions of my silence. I am part of Guillaumet, and Guillaumet is part of me.

I am part of Guillaumet, of Gavoille, of Hochedé, and they are part of me. I am part of Group 2-33, and it of me. I am part of my country, and it of me. My country and I are one. And all the men of Group 2-33 are one with their country.

XXI

I HAVE changed a good deal. I had been bitter these last days, Major Alias—these last days when the armored invasion was meeting no resistance, when our sacrificial offerings cost the Group seventeen out of twenty-three crews. It had seemed to me that we—that you in particular—were agreeing to play the part of dead men merely because the show called for dead supernumeraries. I had been bitter, Major Alias; and I had been wrong.

You in particular, but the rest of us too, had clung to the letter of a duty whose spirit had ceased to be visible for us. You had driven us intuitively not towards victory, which was impossible, but towards self-fulfillment. You knew as well as we did that the intelligence we brought back would never reach the Staff. But you were salvaging rites whose power none of us could perceive. Each time that you examined us on the lorries, the barges, the railway trains we had spotted, examined us as soberly as if our answers could possibly serve a purpose, you seemed to me revoltingly hypocritical. But you were right, Major Alias.

Until I learnt what I learnt over Arras, I could feel no responsibility for this stream of refugees over which once more I fly. I can be bound to no men except those to whom I give. I understand no men except those to whom I am bound. I exist only to the degree that I am nourished by the springs at my roots. I am bound to that mob on the highways, and it is bound to me. At three hundred miles an hour and an elevation of six hundred feet, now that I have come down out of the clouds, I have become one with that mob. I, flying in the descending night, am like a shepherd who in a single glance counts and collects and welds his scattered sheep into a flock again. That mob is no longer a mob, it is a people.

We dwell in the rot of defeat, yet I am filled with a solemn and abiding jubilation, as if I had just come from a sacrament. I am steeped in chaos, yet I have won a victory. Is there a single pilot of the Group who ever flew home without this feeling of victory in his breast? This very day, when Pénicot came in from a morning's low-altitude sortie and was telling me about it, this was how he spoke: "Whenever one of their ground batteries seemed to me to be aiming too well for my comfort, I would zoom down just above the ground and make straight for the battery at full speed, and the spray from my guns would blow out their ruddy fire as if it was a candle. Before they knew it, I was on their gun crew, and you would have thought I was a bursting shell. *Bang!* The crew would scatter and flop in every direction. I swear, I felt as if I was scattering nine-pins." And Pénicot, victorious captain, roared with glee, as pleased with himself as Gavoille's gunner when they flew through the vault of the enemy searchlights like a military wedding-party marching under an arch of swords.

"Ninety-four, captain."

Dutertre had picked up a landmark along the Seine, and we were down now to four hundred feet. Flowing beneath me at three hundred miles an hour, the earth was drawing great rectangles of wheat and alfalfa, great triangles of forest, across my glass windscreen. Divided by the stem of the plane, the flow of the broken landscape to left and right filled me with a curious satisfaction. The Seine shone below, and when I crossed its winding course at an angle it seemed to speed past and pivot upon itself. The swirl of the river was as lovely in my sight as the curve of a sickle in a field. I felt restored to my element. I was captain of my ship. The fuel tanks were holding out. I should certainly win a drink at poker dice from Pénicot and then beat Lacordaire at chess. That was how I was when my team had won.

"Captain! Firing at us! We are in forbidden territory."

Forbidden, that is, by our own people. A rectangle in which our own people fired on any plane, friend or enemy. We had orders to fly round it, but the Group never bothered to observe these traffic regulations. Well, it was Dutertre who set the course, not I. Nobody could blame me.

"Firing hard?"

"Doing as well as they can."

"Want to go back and round?"

"Oh, no."

His tone was matter-of-fact. We had been through our storm. For men like us, this anti-aircraft fire was a mere April shower. Still. . . .

"Dutertre, wouldn't it be silly to be brought down by our own guns?"

"They won't bring anything down. Just giving themselves a little exercise."

Dutertre was in a sarcastic mood. Not I. I was happy. I was impatient to be back with the Group again.

"They are, for a fact. Firing like. . . ."

The gunner! Come to, has he? This is the first time on board that he has opened his mouth without being spoken to. He took in the whole jaunt without feeling the need of speech. Unless that was he who muttered "Boy! oh, boy!" when the shells were thickest. But you wouldn't call that blabbing, exactly. He spoke now because machine guns are his specialty—and how can you keep a specialist quiet about his specialty?

It was impossible for me not to contrast in my mind the two worlds of plane and earth. I had led Dutertre and my gunner this day beyond the bourne at which reasonable men would stop. We had seen France in flames. We had seen the sun shining on the sea. We had grown old in the upper altitudes. We had bent our glance upon a distant earth as over the cases of a museum. We had sported in the sunlight with the dust of enemy fighter planes. Thereafter we had dropped earthward again and flung ourselves into the holocaust. What we could offer up, we had sacrificed. And in that sacrifice we had learnt even more about ourselves than we should have done after ten years in a monastery. We had come forth again after ten years in a monastery.

And in the little time we had taken to wander so far, the caravan of refugees over which we flew had perhaps advanced five hundred yards. In less time than it would take them to lift a motorcar out of a ditch and set it back on the road again, in less time than many a driver would sit drumming impatiently on the wheel as he waited for a stream of traffic to empty itself out of a crossroad, we should be safely back in our haven.

At a single bound we had leapt over the whole defeat. We were above and beyond it, pilgrims stronger than the desert through which they toil because already in their hearts they have reached the holy city that is their destination. This night now falling would park that unhappy people of refugees in its stable of misery. The flock would huddle together for comfort, but to whom, to what would it cry out? Whereas we fly towards comrades and a kind of celebration. A lamplight gleaming from the humblest hut can change the rudest winter night into Christmas Eve. We in this plane are bound for a place where there will be comrades to welcome us. We in this plane are bound for the communion of our daily bread.

Sufficient unto this day is the weariness and the bliss thereof. I shall turn over to the ground crew my ship made noble by her scars. I shall strip off my cumbrous flying clothes; and as it is now too late to win that drink from Pénicot, I shall go directly to table and dine among my comrades. We are late. Those who are late never get back. Late, are they? If late, then too late. Then nothing can be done for them. The night has swung them into eternity.

Yet at the dinner hour, when the Group takes a census of its dead, one thing is done for them: they are made handsomer than was their wont. They are sketched for ever in their most luminous smile. But we in this plane are surrendering that privilege. We shall surge up out of nowhere, like demons, like poachers in a wood. The major's hand will stop with his bread half way to his mouth. He will stare at us. Perhaps he will say, "Oh! . . . Oh, there you are!" The rest will say nothing. They will scarcely throw us a glance.

There was a time when I had small respect for grown-ups. I was wrong. Men do not really grow old. Men are as pure when you come back to them as when you left them. "Oh, there you are, you who are of our kind!" The words thought and not spoken, out of delicacy of feeling.

Major Alias, that communion of spirit with the Group was to me as is the fire in the hearth to the blind. The blind sit down and put forth their palms, not seeing the source of the gladness they feel. We come home from our sortie ready for our silent reward. Its quality is unique, for it is the quality of love. We do not recognize it as love. Love, when ordinarily we think of it, implies a more tumultuous pathos. But this is the veritable love—a web woven of strands in which we are fulfilled.

XXII

WHEN I got back to my billet I found my farmer at table with his wife and niece.

"Tell me," I said to him; "how many instruments do you think a pilot has to look after?"

"How should I know? Not my trade," he answered. "Must be some missing, though, to my way of thinking. The ones you win a war with. Have some supper?"

I said I'd had supper at the mess, but already he wasn't listening to me.

"You, our niece, there. Shove along a little. Make room for the captain."

I was made to sit down between the girl and her aunt. Here was something besides the Group that I formed part of. Through my comrades I was woven into the whole of my country. Love is a seed: it has only to sprout, and its roots spread far and wide.

Silently my farmer broke the bread and handed it

round. Unruffled, austere, the cares of his day had clothed him in dignity. Perhaps for the last time at this table, he shared his bread with us as in an act of worship. I sat thinking of the wide fields out of which that substance had come. To-morrow those fields would be invaded by the enemy. Oh, there would be no tumult of men and clashing arms! The earth is vast. My farmer would see no more of the invasion than a solitary sentinel posted against the wide sky on the edge of the fields. In appearance nothing would have changed; but a single sign is enough to tell man that everything has changed.

The wind running through the field of grain will still resemble a wind running over the sea. But the wind in the grain is a more wonderful sweep, for as it ruffles the tips of the wheat it takes a census of a patrimony. It takes stock of a future. The wind in the grain is the caress to the spouse, it is the hand of peace stroking her hair.

To-morrow that wheat will have changed. Wheat is something more than carnal fodder. To nourish man is not the same as to fatten cattle. Bread has more than one meaning. We have learnt to see in bread a means of communion between men, for men break bread together. We have learnt to see in bread the symbol of the dignity of labor, for bread is earned in the sweat of the brow. We have learnt to see in bread the essential vessel of compassion, for it is bread that is distributed to the miserable. There is no savour like that of bread shared between men. And I saw of a sudden that the energy contained in this spiritual food, this bread of the spirit generated by that field of wheat, was in peril. To-morrow, perhaps, when he broke bread again and sent it round the table, my farmer would not be celebrating the same household rite. To-morrow, perhaps, his bread would not bring the same glow into these faces round the table. For bread is like the oil of the lamp: its merit is in the light it sheds.

I looked at the beautiful niece beside me and said to myself, "Bread, in this child, is transmuted into languid grace. It is transmuted into modesty. It is transmuted into gentle silence. And to-morrow, perhaps, this same bread, by virtue of a single gray blot rising on the edge of that ocean of wheat, though it nourish this same lamp, will perhaps no longer send forth this same glowing light. The power that is in this bread will have gone out of it."

I had made war this day to preserve the glowing light in that lamp, and not to feed that body. I had made war for the particular radiation into which bread is trans-muted in the homes of my countrymen. What moved me so deeply in that pensive little girl was the insub-stantial vestment of the spirit. It was the mysterious to-tality composed by the features of her face. It was the poem on the page, more than the page itself.

The little girl felt that I was looking at her. She raised her eyes to mine. It seemed to me that she smiled at me. Her smile was hardly more than a breath over the face

"That book might have made them look upon me as an outsider, yet it didn't. I was still one of them." (PAGE 195)

of the waters; but that fugitive gleam was enough. I was moved. I felt, mysteriously present, a soul that belonged in this place and other. There was a peace here, sensing which I murmured to myself, "The peace of the kingdom of silence." That smile was the glow of the shining wheat.

The face of the niece was unruffled again, veiling its unfathomable depth. The farmer's wife sighed, looked round at us, and spoke no word. The farmer, his mind on the day to come, sat wrapped in his earthy wisdom. Behind the silence of these three beings there was an inner abundance that was like the patrimony of a whole village asleep in the night—and like it, threatened. Strange, the intensity with which I felt myself responsible for that invisible patrimony. I went out of the house to walk alone on the highway, and I carried with me a burden that seemed to me tender and in no wise heavy, like a child asleep in my arms.

I walked slowly, not caring where I went. I had promised myself this conversation with my village; but now I found that I had nothing to say. I was like that heavily laden bough that had flashed into my mind when the sense of victory had swelled in me. I strolled and lingered, filled with the thought of the ties that bound me to my people. I was one with them, they were one with me. That farmer handing round the bread had made no gift to us at table: he had shared with us and exchanged with us that bread in which all of us had our part. And by that sharing the farmer had not been impoverished but enriched. He had eaten sweeter bread, bread of the community, by that sharing. And I, when I took off for France this afternoon, had made no gift either. We of the Group gave nothing to our people. We were their part in the sacrifice of war. Seeing this, I could see why Hochedé fought the war without mouth-filling words, flew his sorties like a blacksmith working at his smithy. "Who are you?"—"I am the village blacksmith." The blacksmith is serene.

I strolled and lingered on the highway, filled with hope among those who seemed to be hopeless; yet even in this I was not cut off from the rest. I was their part in hope. True, we were already beaten. True, all was in suspense. True, all was threatened. Yet despite this, I could not but feel in myself the serenity of victory. Contradiction in terms? I don't give a fig for terms. I was like Pénicot, Hochedé, Alias, Gavoille. Like them, I had no language by which to justify my feeling of victory. But like them I was filled with the sense of my responsibility. And what man can feel himself at one and the same time responsible and hopeless?

Defeat. . . . Victory. . . . Terms I do not know what to make of. One victory exalts, another corrupts. One defeat kills, another brings life. Tell me what seed is lodged in your victory or your defeat, and I will tell you its future. Life is not definable by situations but by mutations. There is but one victory that I know is sure, and that is the victory that is lodged in the energy of the seed. Sow the seed in the wide black earth and already the seed is victorious, though time must contribute to the triumph of the wheat.

This morning France was a shattered army and a chaotic population. But if in a chaotic population there is a single consciousness animated by a sense of responsibility, the chaos vanishes. A rock pile ceases to be a rock pile the moment a single man contemplates it, bearing within him the image of a cathedral. I shall not fret about the loam if somewhere in it a seed lies buried. The seed will drain the loam and the wheat will blaze.

He who accedes to contemplation transmutes himself into seed. He who makes a discovery pulls me by the sleeve to draw my attention to it. He who invents preaches his invention. How a Hochedé will express himself or act, I do not know, nor does it matter. He will surely spread his tranquil faith. What I do see more clearly now is the prime agent of victory. He who bears in his heart a cathedral to be built is already victorious. He who seeks to become sexton of a finished cathedral is already defeated. Victory is the fruit of love. Only love can say what face shall emerge from the clay. Only love can guide man towards that face. Intelligence is valid only as it serves love.

The sculptor is great with the burden of his creation. It matters little that he know not how he will draw it forth from the clay. From one thumb stroke to the next, from error to error, contradiction to contradiction, he will move through the clay towards his creation. Intelligence is not creative; judgment is not creative. If the sculptor be but skill and mind, his hands will be without genius.

Concerning the part played by intelligence, we were long in error. We neglected the substance of man. We believed that the virtuosity of base natures could aid in the triumph of noble causes, that shrewd selfishness could exalt spirits to sacrifice, that withered hearts could by a wind of phrases found brotherhood or love. We neglected Being. The seed of the cedar will become cedar. The seed of the bramble can only become bramble. I shall no longer content myself with judging men according to the phrases by which they justify their acts. I shall no longer accept as gold the bond they put up in the form of words, nor be deceived concerning the direction in which their acts tend. Here is a man striding towards his home: I cannot say if he is going towards quarrel or towards love. I can ask myself only this: "What sort of man is he?" And when I know that, only then shall I know by what lodestone he is impelled, and where he is bound. For in the end man always gravitates in the direction commanded by the lodestone within him.

The seed haunted by the sun never fails to find its way between the stones in the ground. And the pure logician, if no sun draws him forth, remains entangled in his logic. I shall not forget the lesson taught me by my enemy himself. What direction should the armored column take to invest the rear of the enemy? Nobody can say. What should the armored column be for this purpose? It should be weight of sea pressing against dike. What ought we do? This. That. The contrary of this or that. There is no determinism that governs the future. What ought we be? That is the essential question, the question that concerns spirit and not intelligence. For spirit impregnates intelligence with the creation that is to come forth. And later, intelligence is brought to bed of creation. How should man go about building the first ship ever known? Very complicated, this. The ship will be born of a thousand errors and fumblings. But what should man be to build that first ship? Here I seize the problem of creation at the root. Merchant. Soldier. In love with the prospect of faraway lands. For then of necessity designers and builders will be born of that love. They will drain the energy of workmen and one day launch a ship. What should we do to annihilate a forest? The question is not easy. What be? Obviously, a forest fire.

To-morrow we of France will enter into the night of defeat. May my country still exist when day dawns again. What ought we do to save my country? I do not know. Contradictory things. Our spiritual heritage must be preserved, else our people will be deprived of their genius. Our people must be preserved else our heritage will become lost. For want of a way to reconcile heritage and people in their formulas, logicians will be tempted to sacrifice either the body or the soul. But I want nothing to do with logicians. I want my country to exist both in the flesh and in the spirit when day dawns. Therefore I must bear with all the weight of my love in that direction. There is no passage the sea cannot clear for itself if it bear with all its weight.

The blind move towards the fire in the hearth because the need of that fire is in them. At a distance, they are already governed by it. They seek it because already they have found it. The sculptor guided by the need to mould the clay is already in possession of his creation. And we of the Group are like that. We are warmed by the awareness of the ties that bind us to our people— wherefore we feel ourselves already victorious. We know that we are one with the rest. But that the rest may know it, we must learn to express it. That is a matter of consciousness and language. A matter also of avoiding the verbal traps of superficial logic and polemical wrangling in which substance is destroyed. Above all we must not reject any part of that to which we belong.

And therefore I, leaning back against a wall in the silence of the village night, home from my flight to Arras, enlightened, as it seemed to me, by my flight to Arras, imposed upon myself these rules that I shall never betray.

Since I am one with the people of France, I shall never reject my people, whatever they may do. I shall never preach against them in the hearing of others. Whenever it is possible to take their defence, I shall defend them. If they cover me with shame I shall lock up that shame in my heart and be silent. Whatever at such a time I shall think of them, I shall never bear witness against them. Does a husband go from house to house crying out to his neighbours that his wife is a strumpet? Is it thus that he can preserve his honour? No, for his wife is one with his home. No, for he cannot establish his dignity against her. Let him go home to her, and there unburden himself of his anger.

Thus, I shall not divorce myself from a defeat which surely will often humiliate me. I am part of France, and France is part of me. France brought forth men called Pascal, Renoir, Pasteur, Guillaumet, Hochedé. She brought forth also men who were inept, were politicasters, were cheats. But it would be too easy for a man to declare himself part of the first France and not of the other.

Defeat divides men. Defeat unbinds that which was bound. In this unbinding there is danger of death. I shall not contribute to these divisions between Frenchmen by casting the responsibility for the disaster upon those of my people who think differently from me. Where there is no judge, nothing is to be gained by hurling accusations. All Frenchmen were defeated together. I was defeated. Hochedé was defeated. Hochedé does not blame others for the defeat. Hochedé says to himself, "I, Hochedé, who am one with France, was weak. France that is one with me, Hochedé, was weak. I was weak in her, and she in me." Hochedé knows perfectly that once he begins distinguishing between his people and himself, he glorifies only himself. And from that moment there ceases to exist a Hochedé who is part of a home, a family, a Group, a nation: there remains a Hochedé who is part of a desert.

If I take upon myself a share in my family's humiliation I shall be able to influence my family. It is part of me, as I am of it. But if I reject its humiliation, my family must collapse; and I shall wander alone, filled with vainglory, but a shell as empty as a corpse.

I reject non-being. My purpose is to be. And if I am to be, I must begin by assuming responsibility. Only a few hours ago I was blind. I was bitter. But now I am able to judge more clearly. Just as I refuse to complain of other Frenchmen, since now I feel myself one with France, so I am no longer able to conceive that France has the right to complain of the rest of the world. Each is responsible for all. France was responsible for all the world. Had France been France, she might have stood to the world as the common ideal round which the world would have rallied. She might have served as the keystone in the world's arch. Had France possessed the flavour of France, the radiation of France, the whole world would have been magnetized into a resistance of which the spearhead would have been France. I reject henceforth my reproaches against the world. Assuming that at a given moment the world lacked a soul, France owed it to herself to serve as the world's soul.

France, too, had need to avoid non-being, and to be. There was a time when my Group volunteered for service elsewhere against aggression—in Norway, and again in Finland. What were Norway and Finland, I used to wonder, to the soldiers and petty officers of France? And I would say to myself that in some confused way those men were volunteering to die in a human cause symbolized by mental images of snow and Christmas sleigh-bells. The salvaging of that particular flavour in the world seemed to justify, in their eyes, the sacrifice of their lives. Had we of France meant a kind of Christmas to the world, the world would have been saved through our being.

The spiritual communion of men the world over did not operate in our favour. But had we stood for that communion of men, we should have saved the world and ourselves. In that task we failed. Each is responsible for all. Each is by himself responsible. Each by himself is responsible for all. I understand now for the first time the mystery of the religion whence was born the civilization I claim as my own: "To bear the sins of man." Each man bears the sins of all men.

XXIII

WHO would call this a creed for the weak? A chief is a man who assumes responsibility. He says, "I was beaten." He does not say, "My men were beaten." Thus speaks a real man. Hochedé would say, "I was responsible."

I know the meaning of humility. It is not self-disparagement. It is the motive power of action. If, intending to absolve myself, I plead fate as the excuse for my misfortunes, I subject myself to fate. If I plead treason as their excuse, I subject myself to treason. But if I accept responsibility, I affirm my strength as a man. I am able to influence that of which I form part. I declare myself a constituent part of the community of mankind.

Thus there is a creature within me against whom I struggle in order that I may rise superior to myself. Except for that flight to Arras I should never have been able to distinguish between that creature and the man I seek to be. A metaphor comes into my mind. What it is worth, I do not know, but here it is: the individual is a mere path. What matters is Man, who takes that path.

The kind of truth advanced in verbal bickerings can no longer satisfy me. I know now that the freezing of my controls is not to be explained by the negligence of government clerks, nor the absence of friendly nations at the side of France by the egoism of those nations. It is true that we can explain defeat by pointing to the incapacity of specific individuals. But a civilization is a thing that kneads and moulds men. If the civilization to which I belong was brought low by the incapacity of individuals, then my question must be, why did my civilization not create a different type of individual?

A civilization, like a religion, accuses itself when it complains of the tepid faith of its members. Its duty is to indue them with fervor. It accuses itself when it complains of the hatred of other men not its members. Its duty is to convert those other men. Yet there was a time when my civilization proved its worth—when it inflamed its apostles, cast down the cruel, freed peoples enslaved—though to-day it can neither exalt nor convert. If what I seek is to dig down to the root of the many causes of my defeat; if my ambition is to be born anew, I must begin by recovering the animating power of my civilization, which has become lost.

For what is true of wheat is true also of a civilization. Wheat nourishes man, but man in turn preserves wheat from extinction by storing up its seed. The seed stored up is a kind of heritage received by one generation of wheat after another. If wheat is to flourish in my fields, it is not enough that I be able to describe it and desire it. I must possess the seed whence it springs. And so with my civilization, for it too springs from energy contained within a seed. If what I wish is to preserve on earth a given type of man, and the particular energy that radiates from him, I must begin by salvaging the principles that animate that kind of man.

My civilization had ceased to be radiant energy. I was able to describe it glibly enough; but I had lost sight of the principle that animated it and bore it along through the ages. And what I have learnt this night is that the words I used to describe my civilization never went to the heart of the matter. Thus I have preached Democracy, for example, without the least notion that, in respect of the qualities and destiny of Man, I was merely giving expression to an aggregate of wishes and not an aggregate of principles. I wished man to be fraternal, free, and strong. Of course! Who would not wish the same? I was able to describe how man ought to act—but not what he ought to be. I used words like mankind, but without defining them. The idea of a community of men seemed to me natural and self-evident. But what is there natural and self-evident about it? The moral climate I had in mind is not natural—it is the product of a particular architecture. A fascist band, a slave market is a community of men—of a sort.

As for my community of men, I waited until I was in jeopardy before I took thought of it. As soon as danger threatened, I took shelter behind it. "What!" I cried. "Are you not ashamed to attack such a beautiful cathedral!" But I had long ceased to be the architect of that cathedral. I had been living in it as sexton, as beadle. Which is to say, as a man defeated in advance. I had been taking advantage of its tranquillity, its tolerance, its warmth. I had been a parasite upon it. It had meant to me no more than a place where I was snug and secure, like a passenger on a ship. The passenger makes use of the ship and gives it nothing in return. The ship is to him a water-tight playground. He is indifferent to the straining of the timbers against the ceaseless hostility of the sea. How he would cry out if the ship were capsized by a storm! But what has he sacrificed to the ship? If the members of my civilization have degenerated, and if I have been defeated, against whom am I to lodge a complaint?

There exists a common denominator that integrates all the qualities I demand in the men of my civilization. There exists a keystone that sustains the arch of the particular community which men are called to found. There exists a principle, an animating force, out of which everything once emerged—root, trunk, branches, fruit. That principle was once a radiating seed in the

loam of mankind. Only by it can I be made victorious.
What is it?

It seemed to me that I was learning many things in
the course of my strange village night. There was
something extraordinary in the quality of its silence.
The least sound filled all space like a bell. Nothing existed that was not part of me—neither the moaning of
the cattle, nor a sudden distant cry, nor the sound of
a door as it shut. Each little happening seemed to happen within me, and each stirred up a feeling so poignant
that I sought to seize it and fix it before it could vanish.

"That gun-fire over Arras," I said to myself. It had
cracked my stubborn shell, and I was released. Within
that shell, I must have been setting my house in order
the whole day through. I had been the grumbling agent
of an absentee landlord. I had been, in other words, an
individual. And then Man had appeared. Very simply,
he had taken the place of the individual within me.
He had sent one look down upon that mob on the
highway, and had seen in that mob a people. His people.
Man, the common denominator uniting me with that
people. Because Man inhabited me I had flown home-
ward to the Group with the feeling that I was hurrying
to a fire in a hearth. Because Man was looking at men
through my eyes—Man, the common denominator of
all comrades.

Was it a sign? I was so ready to believe in signs. The
night was filled with an apprehension of tacit concord.

Each sound reached me like a message at once limpid and obscure. I heard suddenly the footsteps of a man on his way home.

"Good evening, Captain."

"Good evening."

I did not know the man. We were like two fishermen hailing each other from bark to bark. Yet once again I sensed the existence of a miraculous relationship. Man, dwelling this night within me, would never make an end of counting his own. Man, the common denominator of peoples and nations.

That man was on his way home with his budget of cares and ruminations and images. With his own cargo locked up within himself. I might have gone up to him and spoken. On the white strip of a village street we might have exchanged a few of our memories. So merchants on the way home from faraway lands used to exchange treasures when they met.

In my civilization, he who is different from me does not impoverish me—he enriches me. Our unity is constituted in something higher than ourselves—in Man. When we of Group 2-33 argue of an evening, our arguments do not strain our fraternity, they reënforce it. For no man seeks to hear his own echo, or to find his reflection in the glass. Staring into the glass called Man, the Frenchman of France sees the Norwegian of Norway; for Man heightens and absorbs them both, finds room in himself for the customs of the French as easily as for the manners of the Norwegians. Tales of snow

*"Those who are late never get back . . . The
night has swung them into eternity."*

(PAGE 209)

are told in Norway, tulips are grown in Holland, flamencos are sung in Spain—and we, participating in Man, are enriched by them all. This, perhaps, was why my Group longed and volunteered to fight for Norway.

And now I seem to have come to the end of a long pilgrimage. I have made no discovery. Like a man waking out of sleep, I am once again looking at that to which I had for so long been blind. I see now that in my civilization it is Man who holds the power to bind into unity all the individual diversities. There is in Man, as in all beings, something more than the mere sum of the materials that went to his making. A cathedral is a good deal more than the sum of its stones. It is geometry and architecture. The cathedral is not to be defined by its stones, since those stones have no meaning apart from the cathedral, receive from it their sole significance. And how diverse the stones that have entered into this unity! The most grimacing of the gargoyles are easily absorbed into the canticle of the cathedral.

But the significance of Man, in whom my civilization is summed up, is not self-evident: it is a thing to be taught. There is in mankind no natural predisposition to acknowledge the existence of Man, for Man is not made evident by the mere existence of men. It is because Man exists that we are men, not the other way round. My civilization is founded upon the reverence for Man present in all men, in each individual. My civilization has sought through the ages to reveal Man to men, as it might have taught us to perceive the cathedral in a mere heap of stones. This has been the text of its sermon—that Man is higher than the individual.

And this, the true significance of my civilization, is what I had little by little forgotten. I had thought that it stood for a sum of men as stone stands for a sum of stones. I had mistaken the sum of stones for the cathedral, wherefore little by little my heritage, my civilization, had vanished. It is Man who must be restored to his place among men. It is Man that is the essence of our culture. Man, the keystone in the arch of the community. Man, the seed whence springs our victory.

It is easy to establish a society upon the foundation of rigid rules. It is easy to shape the kind of man who submits blindly and without protest to a master, to the precepts of a Koran. The real task is to succeed in setting man free by making him master of himself.

But what do we mean by setting man free? You cannot free a man who dwells in a desert and is an unfeeling brute. There is no liberty except the liberty of some one making his way towards something. Such a man can be set free if you will teach him the meaning of thirst, and how to trace a path to a well. Only then will he embark upon a course of action that will not be without significance. You could not liberate a stone if there were no law of gravity—for where will the stone go, once it is quarried?

My civilization sought to found human relations upon the belief in Man above and beyond the individual, in order that the attitude of each person towards himself and towards others should not be one of blind conformity to the habits of the ant-hill, but the free expression of love. The invisible path of gravity liberates the stone. The invisible slope of love liberates man. My civilization sought to make every man the ambassador of their common prince. It looked upon the individual as the path or the message of a thing greater than himself. It pointed the human compass towards magnetized directions in which man would ascend to attain his freedom.

I know how this field of energy came to be. For centuries my civilization contemplated God in the person of man. Man was created in the image of God. God was revered in Man. Men were brothers in God. It was this reflection of God that conferred an inalienable dignity upon every man. The duties of each towards himself and towards his kind were evident from the fact of the relations between God and man. My civilization was the inheritor of Christian values.

It was the contemplation of God that created men who were equal, for it was in God that they were equal. This equality possessed an unmistakable significance. For we cannot be equal except we be equal *in* something. The private and the captain are equal in the Nation. Equality is a word devoid of meaning if nothing exists in which it can be expressed.

This equality in the rights of God—rights that are inherent in the individual—forbade the putting of obstacles in the way of the ascension of the individual; and I understand why. God had chosen to adopt the individual as His path. But as this choice also implied the equality of the rights of God "over" the individual, it was clear that individuals were themselves subjected to common duties and to a common respect for law. As the manifestation of God, they were equal in their rights. As the servants of God, they were also equal in their duties.

I understand why an equality that was founded upon God involved neither contradiction nor disorder. Demagogy enters at the moment when, for want of a common denominator, the principle of equality degenerates into a principle of identity. At that moment the private refuses to salute the captain, for by saluting the captain he is no longer doing honor to the Nation, but to the individual.

As the inheritor of God, my civilization made men equal in Man.

I understand the origin of the respect of men for one another. The scientist owed respect to the stoker, for what he respected in the stoker was God; and the stoker, no less than the scientist, was an ambassador of God.

However great one man may be, however insignificant another, no man may claim the power to enslave another. One does not humble an ambassador. And yet this respect for man involved no degrading prostration before the insignificance of the individual, before brutishness or ignorance—since what was honored was not the individual himself but his status as ambassador of God. Thus the love of God founded relations of dignity between men, relations between ambassadors and not between mere individuals.

As the inheritor of God, my civilization founded the respect for Man present in every individual.

I understand the origin of brotherhood among men. Men were brothers in God. One can be a brother only *in* something. Where there is no tie that binds men, men are not united but merely lined up. One cannot be a brother to nobody. The pilots of Group 2-33 are brothers in the Group. Frenchmen are brothers in France.

As the inheritor of God, my civilization made men to be brothers in Man.

I understand the meaning of the duties of charity which were preached to me. Charity was the service of God performed through the individual. It was a thing owed to God, however insignificant the individual who was its recipient. Charity never humiliated him who profited from it, nor ever bound him by the chains of gratitude, since it was not to him but to God that the gift was made. And the practice of charity, meanwhile, was never at any time a kind of homage rendered to insignificance, to brutishness, or to ignorance. The physician owed it to himself to risk his life in the care of a plague-infested nobody. He was serving God thereby. He was never a lesser man for having spent a sleepless night at the bedside of a thief.

As the inheritor of God, my civilization made charity to be a gift to Man present in the individual.

I understand the profound meaning of the humility exacted from the individual. Humility did not cast down the individual, it raised him up. It made clear to him his role as ambassador. As it obliged him to respect the presence of God in others, so it obliged him to respect the presence of God in himself, to make himself the messenger of God or the path taken by God. It forced him to forget himself in order that he might wax and grow; for if the individual exults in his own importance, the path is transformed into a sea.

As the inheritor of God, my civilization preached self-respect, which is to say respect for Man present in oneself.

I understand, finally, why the love of God created men responsible for one another and gave them hope as a virtue. Since it made of each of them the ambassador of the same God, in the hands of each rested the salvation of all. No man had the right to despair, since each was the messenger of a thing greater than himself. Despair was the rejection of God within oneself. The duty of hope was translatable thus: "And dost thou think thyself important? But thy despair is self-conceit!"

As the inheritor of God, my civilization made each responsible for all, and all responsible for each. The individual was to sacrifice himself in order that by his sacrifice the community be saved; but this was no matter of idiotic arithmetic. It was a matter of the respect for Man present in the individual. What made my civilization grand was that a hundred miners were called upon to risk their lives in the rescue of a single miner entombed. And what they rescued in rescuing that miner was Man.

I understand by this bright light the meaning of liberty. It is liberty to grow as the tree grows in the field of energy of its seed. It is the climate permitting the ascension of Man. It is like a favorable wind. Only by the grace of the wind is the bark free on the waters.

A man built in this wise disposes of the power of the tree. What space may his roots not cover! What human pulp may he not absorb to grow and blossom in the sun!

But I had ruined everything. I had dissipated the inheritance. I had allowed the notion of Man to rot.

And yet my civilization had expended a good share of its genius and its energy to preserve the cult of a Prince revealed in the existence of individual men, and the high quality of human relations established by that cult. All the efforts of Humanism tended towards this end in the age of the Renaissance and after. Humanism assigned to itself the exclusive mission of brightening and perpetuating the ideal of the primacy of Man over the individual. What Humanism preached was Man.

But as soon as we seek to speak of Man, our language displays itself insufficient. Man is not the same as men. We say nothing essential about the cathedral when we speak of its stones. We say nothing essential about Man when we seek to define him by the qualities of men. Humanism strove in a direction blocked in advance when it sought to seize the notion of Man in terms of logic and ethics, and by these terms communicate that notion to the human consciousness. Unity of being is not communicable in words. If I knew men to whom the notion of the love of country or of home was strange, and I sought to teach them the meaning of these words, I could not summon a single argument that would waken the sense of country or home in them. I may, if I like, speak of a farm by referring to its fields, its streams, its pastures, its cattle. Each of these by itself, and all of them together, contribute to the existence of the farm. Yet in that farm there must be something which escapes material analysis, since there are farmers who are ready to ruin themselves for their farms. And it is that "something else" which is the essence of the farm and enhances the particles of which the farm is composed. The cattle, by that something else, become the cattle of a farm, the meadows the meadows of a farm, the fields the fields of a farm.

Thus man becomes the man of a country, of a group, of a craft, of a civilization, of a religion. But if we are to clothe ourselves in these higher beings we must begin by creating them within ourselves. The being of which we claim to form part is created within us not by words but only by acts. A being is not subject to the empire of language, but only to the empire of acts. Our Humanism neglected acts. Therefore it failed in its attempt.

The essential act possesses a name. Its name is sacrifice.

Sacrifice signifies neither amputation nor repentance. It is in essence an act. It is the gift of oneself to the being of which one forms part. Only he can understand what a farm is, what a country is, who shall have sacrificed part of himself to his farm or country, fought to save it, struggled to make it beautiful. Only then will the love of farm or country fill his heart. A country— or a farm—is not the sum of its parts. It is the sum of its gifts.

So long as my civilization leant upon God it was able to preserve the notion of sacrifice whereby God is created in the hearts of men. Humanism neglected the essential role of sacrifice. It thought itself able to communicate the notion of Man by words and not by acts. In order to save the vision of Man present in all men, it could do no more than capitalize the word. And mankind was meanwhile moving down a dangerous slope—for we were in danger of mistaking the average of mankind or the arithmetical sum of mankind for Man. We were in danger of mistaking the sum of the stones for the cathedral. Wherefore little by little we lost our heritage.

Instead of affirming the rights of Man present in the individual we had begun to talk about the rights of the collectivity. We had bit by bit introduced a code for the collectivity which neglected the existence of Man. That code explains clearly why the individual should sacrifice himself for the community. It does not explain clearly and without ambiguity why the community should sacrifice itself for a single member. Why it is equitable that a thousand die to deliver a single man from unjust imprisonment. We still remember vaguely that this should be, but progressively we forget it more and more. And yet it is this principle alone which differentiates us from the ant-hill and which is the source of the grandeur of mankind. For want of an effective concept of humanity—which can rest only upon Man—we have been slipping gradually towards the ant-hill, whose definition is the mere sum of the individuals it contains.

What did we possess that we could set up against the religions of the State and of the Party? What had become of our great ideal of Man born of God? That ideal is scarcely recognizable now beneath the vocabulary of windy words that covers it.

Little by little forgetting man, we limited our code to the problems of the individual. We have gone on preaching the equality of men. But having forgotten Man, we no longer knew what it was we were preaching. Having forgotten in what men were equal, we enunciated a vague affirmation that was of no use to us. How can there be any material equality between individuals as such—the sage and the brute, the imbecile and the genius? On the material plane, equality implies that all men are identical and occupy the same place in the community; which is absurd. Wherefore the principle of equality degenerates and becomes the principle of identity.

We have gone on preaching the liberty of men. But having forgotten Man, we have defined our liberty as a sort of vague license limited only at the point where one man does injury to another. This seeming ideal is devoid of meaning, for in fact no man can act without involving other men. If I, being a soldier, mutilate myself, I am shot. An isolated individual does not exist. He who is sad, saddens others.

And even liberty of this sort had to be subjected to a thousand subterfuges before we could make use of it.

We found it impossible to say when this right was valid and when it was not valid, and as we wanted very much to preserve the vague principle of the thing from the innumerable assaults which every society necessarily makes upon the liberty of the individual, we turned hypocrite and shut our eyes.

As for charity, we have not even dared go on preaching it. There was a time when the sacrifice which created beings took the name of charity each time that it honored God in His image upon earth. By our charity to the individual we made our gift to God, and later to Man. But having forgotten both God and Man, we found ourselves giving only to the individual. And from that moment charity became an unacceptable course. It is society and not the mood of the individual that should ensure equity in the sharing of the goods of this world. The dignity of the individual demands that he be not reduced to vassalage by the largesse of others. What a paradox—that men who possessed wealth should claim the right, over and above their possessions, to the gratitude of those who were without possessions!

But above all our miscomprehended charity turned against its own goal. It was founded exclusively upon feelings of pity with regard to individuals—wherefore it forbade us all educative chastisement. But true charity, being the practice of the rites rendered to Man over and above the individual, taught that the individual must be fought in order that Man grow great.

And thus Man became lost to us. And losing Man we emptied all warmth out of that very fraternity which our civilization had preached to us—since we are brothers *in* something, and not brothers in isolation. It is not by contributions to a pool that fraternity is ensured. Fraternity is the creation of sacrifice alone. It is the creation of the gift made to a thing greater than ourselves. But we, mistaking the very root of all true existence, seeing in it a sterile diminution of our goods, reduced our fraternity to no more than a mutual tolerance of one another.

We ceased to give. Obviously, if I insist upon giving only to myself, I shall receive nothing. I shall be building nothing of which I am to form part, and therefore I shall be nothing. And when, afterwards, you come to me and ask me to die for certain interests, I shall refuse to die. My own interest will command me to live. Where will I find that rush of love that will compensate my death? Men die for a home, not for walls and tables. Men die for a cathedral, not for stones. Men die for a people, not for a mob. Men die for love of Man—provided that Man is the keystone in the arch of their community. Men die only for that by which they live.

The sole reason why our society still seemed a fortunate one, and man seemed still to be distinguishable from the collectivity, was that our true civilization, which we were betraying in our ignorance, still sent forth its dying rays and still, despite ourselves, continued to preserve us.

How was it possible for our enemies to understand this when we ourselves no longer understood it? All that they could see in us was rocks strewn in a field. They sought in their way to lend meaning to the notion of collectivity—a notion we were no longer able to define because we had forgotten the existence of Man. Some of our enemies went straight and lightheartedly away to the most extreme conclusions of logic. Collectivity to them meant an absolute collection. Each stone was to be identical with every other stone. And each stone was to reign alone over itself. This was anarchy; and the anarchists, quite aware of the reverence due to Man, applied its principles rigorously to the individual. The contradictions that were born of that rigor were even greater than those that exist in our society.

Others collected the strewn stones and heaped them up in a field. They preached the rights of the Mass. The formula cannot satisfy; for if it is intolerable that a single man tyrannize a Mass, it is equally intolerable that the Mass oppress a single man.

Still others gathered together those powerless stones and out of their arithmetical sum they formed a State. And their State, too, fails to transcend the men who compose it, is too the mere expression of a sum. It stands for the power of the collectivity delegated into the hands of an individual. It is the reign of one stone—which claims to be identical with the rest—over a heap of stones. This State preaches a code of collective existence which once again we refuse to accept—but towards which, nevertheless, we are slowly moving for want of remembering Man who alone would justify our refusal.

The faithful of that new religion would object to several miners' risking their lives to save a single miner entombed, for in that case the rock pile would be injured. Let one of their wounded seem to be slowing down the advance of their army, and they will finish him off. The good of the community is a thing which they perceive in arithmetic—and it is arithmetic that governs them. They learn by their arithmetic that they would incur loss if they sought to transcend themselves and become greater than they are. Consequently they must hate those who differ from them—since they possess nothing higher than themselves with which to fuse. Every foreign way of life, every foreign race, every foreign system of thought is necessarily an affront to them. They have no power to absorb others, for if we are to convert men to our way we cannot do it by amputating them but must do it by teaching them to express themselves, offering a goal to their aspirations and a territory for the deployment of their energies. To convert is always to set free. A cathedral is able to absorb its stones, which have no meaning but in it. But the rock pile absorbs nothing; and for want of power to absorb, it can only crush. It is not astonishing that a rock pile, with its great weight, possess more power than stones strewn in a field.

And yet it is I who am the stronger.

I am the stronger provided that I am able to find myself. Provided our Humanism restores Man amongst us. Provided we are able to found our community, and, founding it, make use of the sole efficacious instrument —charity. For our community, as it was when our civilization built it, was no mere sum of interests: it was a sum of gifts.

I am the stronger because the tree is stronger than the materials of which it is composed. It drained those materials into itself. It transformed them into itself. The cathedral is more radiant than any heap of stones. I am the stronger because only my civilization possesses the power to bind into its unity all diversity without depriving any element of its individuality.

When I took off for Arras I asked to receive before giving. My demand was in vain. We must give before we can receive, and build before we may inhabit. By my gift of blood over Arras I created the love that I feel for my kind as the mother creates the breast by the gift of her milk. Therein resides the mystery. To create love, we must begin by sacrifice. Afterwards, love will demand further sacrifices and ensure us every victory. But it is we who must take the first step. We must be born before we can exist.

I came back from Arras, having woven my ties with my farmer's family. Through the translucent smile of his niece I saw the wheat of my village. Beyond my village I saw my country, and beyond my country all other countries. I came back to a civilization which had chosen Man as the keystone in its arch. I came back to Group 2-33—that Group that had volunteered to fight for Norway.

I dressed this day for the service of a god to whose being I was blind. Arras unsealed my eyes. Like the others of the Group, I am no longer blind. It may be that to-morrow Alias will order me to fly still another sortie. If, at dawn to-morrow, I fight again, I shall know finally why I fight.

My eyes have been unsealed, and I want now to remember what it is that they have seen. I feel the need of a simple Credo so that I may remember.

I believe in the primacy of Man above the individual and of the universal above the particular.

I believe that the cult of the universal exalts and heightens our particular riches, and founds the sole veritable order, which is the order of life. A tree is an object of order, despite the diversity of its roots and branches.

I believe that the cult of the particular is the cult of death, for it founds its order upon likeness. It mistakes identity of parts for unity of Being. It destroys the cathedral in order to line up the stones. Therefore I shall fight against all those who strive to impose a particular way of life upon other ways of life, a particular people upon other peoples, a particular race upon other races, a particular system of thought upon other systems of thought.

I believe that the primacy of Man founds the only equality and the only liberty that possess significance. I believe in the equality of the rights of Man inherent in every man. I believe that liberty signifies the ascension of Man. Equality is not identity. Liberty is not the exaltation of the individual against Man. I shall fight against all those who seek to subject the liberty of Man either to an individual or to the mass of individuals.

I believe that what my civilization calls charity is the sacrifice granted Man for the purpose of his own fulfillment. Charity is the gift made to Man present in the insignificance of the individual. It creates Man. I shall fight against all those who, maintaining that my charity pays homage to mediocrity, would destroy Man and thus imprison the' individual in an irredeemable mediocrity.

I shall fight for Man. Against Man's enemies—but against myself as well.

XXIV

WE COLLECTED again at midnight to receive orders. Group 2-33 was sleepy. The flame in the fireplace had turned to embers. The Group seemed to be holding up still, but this was an illusion. Hochedé was staring glumly at his precious watch. Pénicot stood against a wall in a corner, his eyes shut. Gavoille, sitting on a table, his glance vacant and legs hanging, was pouting like a child about to cry. The doctor was nodding over a book. Alias alone was still alert, but frighteningly pale, papers before him under the lamplight, discussing something in a low voice with Geley. Discussion, indeed, gives you a false picture. The major was talking. Geley was nodding his head and saying, "Yes, of course." Geley was hanging on to that "Yes, of course" by main strength. He was clinging more and more eagerly to the major's discourse, like a half-drowned man to the neck of a swimmer. Had

I been Alias I should have said without a change of voice, "Captain Geley, you are to be shot at dawn," and waited for the answer.

The Group had not slept for three nights. It stood like a house of cards.

The major got up, went across to Lacordaire, and pulled him out of a dream in which perhaps he was beating me at chess.

"Lacordaire! You take off at dawn. Ground-scraper sortie."

"Very good, major."

"Better get some sleep."

"Yes, major."

Lacordaire sat down again. The major went out, drawing Geley in his wake as if he were a dead fish on the end of a line. It was nearer a week than three days since Geley had been to bed. Like Alias, not only did he fly his sorties, but he carried part of the burden of responsibility for the Group. Human resistance has its limits: Geley seemed to have crossed his. Yet there they were, the swimmer and his burden, going off to the Staff for phantom orders.

Vezin, the skeptical Vezin, asleep on his feet, came teetering over to me like a somnambulist:

"You asleep?"

"I . . ."

I had been lying back in an armchair (for I had found an armchair) and was indeed dropping off. But Vezin's voice bothered me. What was it he had said?

"Looks bad, old boy. . . . Categorically blocked. . . . Looks bad. . . ."

"You asleep?"

"I. . . . No. . . . What looks bad?"

"The war," he said.

That was news, now! I started to drop off again and murmured vaguely, "What war?"

"What do you mean, 'What war'!"

This conversation wasn't going to get very far. Ah, Paula! Had air squadrons been issued with Tyrolian nursemaids we should have been put to bed long ago.

The major flung open the door and called out, "All set! We move out to-night!"

Behind him stood Geley, wide awake. He would put off his "Yes, of course" until to-morrow night. Once again he would somehow find a reserve of strength in himself to help him with the wearying chores of our removal.

The Group got to its feet. The Group said, "Move again? Very good, sir." What else was there to say?

There was nothing to say. We should see to the removal. Lacordaire would stay behind and take off at dawn. If he got back he would meet us at our new base.

There would be nothing to say to-morrow, either. To-morrow, in the eyes of the bystanders, we would be the defeated. The defeated have no right to speak. No more right to speak than has the seed.

THE END

Library of Congress Cataloging-in-Publication Data

Saint-Exupéry, Antoine de, 1900-1944.
[Pilote de guerre. English]
Flight to Arras / Antoine de Saint-Exupéry.
p.   cm. — (Wings of war)
Translation of: Pilote de guerre.
Reprint. Originally published: New York : Reynal & Hitchcock, c1942.
ISBN 0-8094-7970-2 (trade). — ISBN 0-8094-7971-0 (lib. bdg.)
1. Saint-Exupéry, Antoine de, 1900-1944. 2. World War, 1939-1945—Aerial operations, French. 3. World War,
1939-1945—Personal narratives, French. 4. Air pilots, Military—France—Biography. 5. Authors, French—20th
century—Biography. 6. France. Armée de l'air—Biography.
I. Title. II. Series.
D788.S32 1991   940.54'4944'092—dc20 [B]   90-28494 CIP

Published by arrangement with Harcourt Brace Jovanovich, Inc.

Cover photograph © Carl Purcell
Endpapers photograph © Rene Sheret/After Image